Illumination Rounds

Illumination Rounds

Teaching the Literature of the Vietnam War

Larry R. Johannessen
Saint Xavier University

National Council of Teachers of English
1111 Kenyon Road, Urbana, Illinois 61801

Dedicated to the children of the Vietnam generation.

Staff Editor: David A. Hamburg

Cover Illustration: Carlton Bruett

Basic TRIP Design: Michael J. Getz

Interior Design: Doug Burnett

NCTE Stock Number 22728-3050

Library of Congress Cataloging-in-Publication Data

Johannessen, Larry R.
      Illumination rounds: teaching the literature of the Vietnam War / Larry R. Johannessen.
         p.   cm — (Theory & research into practice)
      Includes bibliographical references.
      ISBN 0-8141-2272-8
      1. Vietnamese Conflict, 1961–1975—Literature and the conflict—Study and teaching. 2. American literature—20th century—Study and teaching. 3. War stories, American—Study and teaching.
4. War poetry, American—Study and teaching. I. Title. II. Series.
PS228.V5J6 1992
810.9′358—dc20   91-40482
                                            CIP

Contents

Contents   **vii**

Acknowledgments

I wish to thank Candy Carter, Peter Smagorinsky, and Michael Spooner for their ideas, support, and encouragement; and I especially thank Elizabeth Kahn, without whose insights, critical suggestions, support, and encouragement, this project would not have been possible.

Grateful acknowledgment is also made to the following poets, their representatives, and publishers for permission to reprint copyrighted material: "APO 96225" by Larry Rottmann originally appeared in *Winning Hearts & Minds: War Poems by Vietnam Veterans* (1972), and is reprinted with permission of the author. "Coming Home." From the book, *To Those Who Have Gone Home Tired: New & Selected Poems* by W. D. Ehrhart. Copyright © 1984 by W. D. Ehrhart. Used by permission of the publisher, Thunder's Mouth Press. "Fragment: 5 September 1967" by W. D. Ehrhart. From *Winning Hearts & Minds: War Poems by Vietnam Veterans* (1972). Reprinted by permission of W. D. Ehrhart. "The Man In Black" by Frank A. Cross, Jr. From *Winning Hearts & Minds: War Poems by Vietnam Veterans* (1972). Reprinted by permission of Frank A. Cross, Jr. "The Insert" by R. L. Barth. From *Carrying the Darkness: The Poetry of the Vietnam War*, W. D. Ehrhart, editor, copyright 1985 W. D. Ehrhart. Reprinted by permission of Texas Tech University Press. "Corporal Charles Chungtu, U.S.M.C." by Bryan Alec Floyd. From *The Long War Dead: An Epiphany 1st Platoon, U.S.M.C.* by Bryan Alec Floyd. Published by The Permanent Press, Sag Harbor, New York.

A special thank-you is extended to the Navy Art Collection, Naval Historical Center for permission to use the cover illustration, Steel #26, "Mine on Patrol."

1 Theory and Research

"Teaching about the Vietnam War is not a matter of wanting to recall all the pain; it is a matter of needing to remember, of reaching through our pain to have students see themselves and their world more clearly."

—N. Bradley Christie, "Teaching Our Longest War: Constructive Lessons from Vietnam"

This generation of students is woefully ignorant of America's recent historical and literary past. I did not fully realize this fact until a few years ago. After twelve years of teaching high school, I was in my first semester of full-time college teaching. I knew that students were interested in the Vietnam War and that the college had not previously offered a course on the subject, so I put together a freshman literature course I called "Images of War."

The course was filled before the first day of registration was over. I was certainly correct about student interest in the subject. We spent the first part of the semester studying novels from World Wars I and II, and then I started my unit on Vietnam War literature. We studied some poetry and short stories, and we were just beginning James Webb's (1978) novel *Fields of Fire*, when the following incident took place. After class on the day I introduced the novel, a student came up to ask me a question: "I think I understand all this stuff we are reading in the literature," she said, "but what I can't understand is if we lost this war against the Vietnamese, how could we send our athletes there last summer for the Olympics?" Obviously, she had confused Vietnam with South Korea.

It would be one thing if this were an isolated case (or if geography were the only problem students had), but, unfortunately, it is not. I have now taught the course a number of times, and each time, I have been amazed by students' interest in the war and lack of knowledge about it, and I have been equally amazed by how what little they think they know is so distorted. Christie (1989), who has taught the literature of the Vietnam War in both high school and college, argues that one reason for teaching literature dealing with the war is students' fascination with the topic and their "obvious ignorance about it" (35).

Informal surveys of several classes of college freshmen reveal the following findings: (1) five out of seventy-five students reported studying the Vietnam War in their high school American history classes; (2) those who said they studied the war in American history reported spending one to three days on it—none said they spent more than three days of class time on the war; (3) only one student had ever read any Vietnam War literature in an English class in high school, and that student's teacher was a Vietnam veteran; (4) few students had, on their own, read any serious literature dealing with the war; and (5) most of the students had seen a number of Vietnam War movies, usually including the *Rambo* series and *Platoon,* and had viewed one or both of the weekly television series dealing with the war, the most popular being *China Beach.* Clearly, students are not learning about the Vietnam War in school or on their own, and what they are gleaning from popular culture and the media helps explain why what they do know is full of distortions and misinterpretations.

The results of my own informal survey of what students have learned about the war in school have been corroborated by what little research has been done on the subject. Scholars and researchers point out that for many years the Vietnam War and the literature of the Vietnam War have been ignored in most high school classrooms (Ehrhart 1988, Starr 1988a, Johannessen 1990). For example, after examining a number of studies of high school history textbook treatments of the Vietnam War from 1979–1987 and various high school curricula across the country, Starr concluded that "the text-books neglect Vietnam" and it "was being ignored in the schools" (1988b, 29).

While researchers have examined the extent to which the war is being studied by students in high school history classes, no one has attempted to find out to what extent, if at all, the literature of the Vietnam War is being taught in high school English classes. Indirect evidence suggests that, as with history classes, the literature and films of the war are all but ignored in the textbooks and in the schools. At a recent NCTE convention, I examined the most recent secondary anthologies by major publishers—six different anthologies—and found only one anthology that contained any literature dealing with the Vietnam War, and it contained but a single short selection.

Undergraduate college readers and anthologies are not much different. My own informal analysis of about twenty of these books revealed that most contain no literature dealing with the Vietnam War. A mere handful of readers contain one selection, and typically, that selection is an excerpt from one of the following two new journalism-style personal narratives: either Tim O'Brien's *If I Die in a Combat Zone* or Michael Herr's *Dispatches*. A few literature anthologies contain one or two of Tim O'Brien's short stories. What was most disturbing to me was that even in theme-oriented textbooks, which often contain a number of selections pertaining to war, there is a noticeable absence of anything dealing with the Vietnam War. The implication one gets from examining these books is that practically nothing of literary value has come out of the Vietnam War.

This situation is somewhat surprising in that, since the mid-1980s, the country has at last been willing to remember the experience of Vietnam. Memorials to Vietnam veterans have been built, ticker-tape parades to honor Vietnam veterans have been held throughout the country, popular films as different as *Rambo II* and *Born on the Fourth of July* have been produced and released, and popular books about the war, including fiction, nonfiction, poetry, drama, memoir, and oral history, have been written and published. In short, as Oldham (1986) points out, the Vietnam War is now a popular item. Yet the Vietnam War is rarely included in most secondary history curricula and textbooks and Vietnam War literature is virtually ignored in widely used secondary anthologies and college readers and anthologies (Johannessen 1990).

Recent events, most notably the Soviet Union's war in Afghanistan and our Persian Gulf War, are telling reminders of the need to deal with the many legacies of the Vietnam War. During the Soviet Union's war in Afghanistan, numerous media stories about the war included at least a mention of Vietnam. In addition, historians and political analysts have made comparisons between the Soviet Union's war in Afghanistan and America's involvement in Vietnam, some suggesting that the Vietnam War is a symbol for the modern war. Even Russian soldiers who were interviewed when they were being withdrawn from Afghanistan talked about the Afghan War as being "Russia's Vietnam."

Most recently, the Persian Gulf War has once again raised the specter of Vietnam. Some critics have suggested that America went to the gulf to exorcise a ghost as much as to win a war. A few days after the end of the war, the president even proclaimed, "We've kicked the Vietnam syndrome once and for all." But have we really? While this statement might be true in terms of reestablishing our national purpose and restoring respect for our military, it ignores some of the other legacies of Vietnam. For me, one of the most telling examples came during one of General Schwarzkopf's briefings near the end of the ground campaign. A reporter had asked him about supplying some numbers of enemy killed, and the general, in obvious anger, said, "This is not a Nintendo game. There are soldiers out there risking their lives." Obviously, even General Schwarzkopf has some concerns that the Persian Gulf War may have created an unrealistic view of what war is really like. Perhaps, rather than saying we have buried the ghosts of Vietnam, we ought to keep remembering its legacies.

WHY TEACH THE LITERATURE OF THE VIETNAM WAR?

Christie (1989) argues that the most obvious reason to teach this generation of students about the Vietnam War is that it is seen by many as the most crucial national experience in modern times. It is our longest and costliest war, and it continues to shape our national policies and our attitudes toward others and ourselves. Students' ignorance about the war, then, would seem to suggest something approaching a national imperative that we teach them about this important experience. Taking this argument a step further, Baker (1981) and others warn that if we continue to ignore issues raised by the war, the end result may well be disaster because, as Goodman (1990) warns, there is nothing to prevent the children of the Vietnam generation from thinking that they can control and limit the effects of war better than those of the Vietnam generation did. One obvious effect of our national amnesia about the Vietnam War is that it has led to this generation's ignorance of its immediate past. Helping our students understand this past will go far in preparing them to deal with the world they will encounter outside of school and in dealing with the aftermath of the war.

Student interest is certainly another reason for having our students read some of the excellent literature of the Vietnam War. Courses on Vietnam on our college campuses remain popular at least in part because students want to know more about the war. In fact, Whitteman (1990) notes that such courses have become "staples of college curriculums" (19).

Wilcox (1988), who uses Vietnam War literature in his own college English classes, argues that teaching this literature provides an opportunity for students to study the historical beginnings, the political and military confusion, and the social, economic, and spiritual costs of America's longest and most unpopular war. In addition, he claims that studying the literature of the war "becomes a series of exercises in critical thinking, a pragmatic and exciting means of empowering students to take responsibility for issues that affect their lives and the future of our planet" (40).

Another important reason for including the literature of the Vietnam War in the English curriculum is that there is now a substantial body of scholarship that places this literature firmly in the context of past literature, as well as pointing out its unique features. In fact, as Wittman (1989) notes in the introduction to her excellent bibliography of the literature of the Vietnam conflict:

> [Scholars] have responded with histories and studies, tracing the major styles and themes and comparing them with those of other wars. These studies no longer comprise only single articles in literary journals but also book-length critiques. Some fine examples are Timothy Lomperis's *Reading the Wind*, William Searle's *Search and Clear*, and James Wilson's *Vietnam in Prose and Film*. Journals such as *Critique* and *Modern Fiction Studies*, among others, have devoted whole issues to the study of Vietnam War literature. (xvii)

There are, of course, many other important articles and book-length studies I would add to her list, such as C.D.B. Bryan's (1984) *Barely Suppressed Screams* and Thomas Myers's (1988) *Walking Point*. Christie (1989) notes that the plethora of resources on this subject should not deter anyone from teaching the war for lack of expertise.

Media-Molded Myths and Images

No other literature presents characters whose views of the world and of war have been so influenced and molded by the media as the literature of the Vietnam War. As Bryan points out, "myths and media images had formed [the soldiers'] ideas about war. They went to Vietnam as innocents" and idealists (1984, 70–71). In a similar manner, our students come to us today molded by "China Beach Party myths" and "Ramboesque shoot 'em-up images" of Hollywood's Vietnam that have not been challenged (Johannessen 1990, 12). Vietnam War literature can teach them the dangers of believing in those myths and images.

Others have also addressed this issue and share my concern. For example, Pratt (1987) and Ehrhart (1988) are concerned that in the absence of teaching about Vietnam, of studying the serious literature of the war, students' knowledge of Vietnam, of history, and of the world they live in is largely determined by Sylvester Stallone's

Rambo and other distorted media images. Wittman (1989) and Herzog (1988) worry that the John Wayne myth that motivated young people to go off to war in Vietnam has merely been transformed by the video generation into its own romantic illusions about war—John Rambo. Having students study the literature of the Vietnam War may help them to evaluate their romanticized views. As Endress points out, through these works students must come to terms with a voice much like their own, a voice that will help them realize that war is not a matter of the sanitized, two-dimensional voice that characterizes media coverage of an event, but a complicated series of events brought to term (1984, 28).

Themes that Speak to Students

"A Lieutenant was flying back to his base near Da Nang and on the deck of the chopper was the dead body of a young Marine. The officer stared at the youth's body and said to nobody in particular, 'God, he looks so young.'

"An ageless gunnery sergeant looked over at the the lieutenant who was barely older than the dead teenager at his feet and said wearily, 'The man's dead—that's as old as you get.'"

—Timothy S. Lowry, *And Brave Men, Too*

Besides helping students see the dangers of believing in media-molded myths and images, I would argue that Vietnam War literature offers students a unique mix of themes which in many ways speak directly to them as, perhaps, no other literature is able to do. Our students often believe in their own invincibility, in the limitless potential of technology, and in their own and America's seemingly unlimited power (Johannessen 1989). The literature of Vietnam can teach them, as Pratt notes in describing some of the major patterns in some of the best literature to come out of the war:

. . . the naivete of Americans who want to do it all and who become viciously destructive in their attempts; the belief by the Vietnamese that the Americans are all-powerful; the debilitating loss of traditional values *on all sides* as the war escalates; the failure of modern technology to conquer a people who are determined to fulfill what they are told is their destiny; the degrading effect of the war on a proud U.S. military; how the Americans' belief in individuality changes to a sense of being part of an unstoppable, impersonal machine; the overwhelming effect of the Vietnam War on the American scene itself; and the inability, regardless of political, moral, or even religious beliefs, for American novelists to make sense out of the madness that creates wars such as Vietnam in the modern, "civilized" world. (1987, 153)

One of the most compelling ways in which the literature of the Vietnam War speaks to students is through the voice of the narrator and the nature of the experience that is the focus of much of the literature. Lawson (1988) points out that scholars now recognize that Vietnam was "our nation's first teen-age war." The average age of the American combatant in Vietnam was 19 years as compared with 26 years for the soldier in World War II (26). Much of the literature of the Vietnam War focuses on the adolescent experience—that of a naive youth who is transformed by his or her experiences—written through the eyes of someone not much older than most high school students. In other words, in many ways this literature seems to students to be written by someone much like themselves, and it seems to be about some of the same kinds of struggles they are facing. Again and again, I hear comments such as the following from my own students in response to the literature and films of the Vietnam War: "These characters sound just like us; they even talk about the same stuff we do"; "Most of those people were my age when they went to Vietnam"; "I couldn't believe how young they looked [in the movie]. That could be me!" "My favorite character is Snake [in James Webb's novel *Fields of Fire*]. He is just like a lot of kids I know"; "I never knew they were all just kids. I mean, most of them are like right out of high school"; "When they are not in combat, they are just like any typical teenager: they talk about fast cars, dating, and rock-and-roll music. But they are just like us because one minute they are teenagers and the next minute they are supposed to be adults and make mature decisions."

Exploring Our Beliefs and Values

"What the best of this work does, I believe, is to liberate us from facts and statistics and to provide us with a much broader and more human perspective on the war."

—Bruce Weigl, *"Reading the Wind": The Literature of the Vietnam War—An Interpretive Critique*

Christie (1989) points out that one criticism he often hears from parents and fellow teachers about teaching the Vietnam War is that it is depressing and even offensive. Why do we want to be reminded of the war, and why do we want our children to have to think about it? Certainly many of the works present events in grim and even gruesome detail. However, the best Vietnam War materials have much more to offer than sensationalism, shallow ideology, and adventure. They offer, as Christie argues, just what you would expect from any great literature—through linguistic and/or visual power and precise artistic control, an elevation of episodes or figures into positive emblems "of memory, of human diversity and yet of human solidarity, of the truly remarkable capacity of the human being to endure" (37).

In other words, studying this literature can help our students to see literature as a mode of human behavior and to understand the need to have values that speak to the importance of every human being. The very nature of war has a way of revealing not only the worst but also the best of what humankind is capable of. This literature reveals the power of art and the human spirit to give meaning to the senselessness and ambiguity of war.

Multiple Curricular Purposes

Another attraction of Vietnam materials is their remarkable diversity. There are nearly five hundred novels to choose from (Wittman 1989), hundreds of short stories and poems, a half dozen or so excellent dramas, thousands of pages of documentaries, narratives, and personal histories, and dozens of films. With such a wide selection of available materials, it is possible to design courses or shorter units to serve any number of curricular needs, interests, or approaches.

For example, Mandel (1988) describes how she used the teenage novel *A Boat to Nowhere* by Maureen Crane Wartski (1980) to help her remedial reading classes, which consisted primarily of Southeast Asian and Hispanic students, to foster an interchange of ideas between the Asian and non-Asian students, integrate reading instruction, and introduce values clarification. The novel she used focuses on the experiences of a Vietnamese family who escapes Vietnam after the fall of Saigon in 1975 to find freedom. Mandel (1988) points out that as our schools become increasingly multicultural, it is important that this type of interaction be pursued in the English curriculum.

More conventional courses or units are also possible. Christie recommends the following organization for a six-to-eight-week unit on the Vietnam War for secondary students:

> **Week 1:** Introduction
>
> Historical background

Vocabulary

Documentary film

Week 2: Poems by Vietnam veterans

Week 3: Drama

Weeks 4, 5, 6:

A personal narrative or oral history

Novel

Optional film showing during week 3 or 4

Final test, paper, and/or other project in last week of unit (1989, 35)

Another possibility is to build an entire course around the literature of the Vietnam War. Oldham (1986) uses the following organization for a semester-long course:

1. Personal narrative

2. Realistic novel

3. Experimental novel

4. New Journalism account

5. Oral history

6. One day each week students view an episode from the PBS Vietnam series "Vietnam: A History."

Wilcox suggests a similar course or unit organization in which the focus is on fiction, nonfiction, and poetry by Vietnam veterans or others who participated in the war (1988, 39–40). Christie's college-level course includes a brief historical perspective on America's involvement in Indochina, and then focuses on imaginative works, including personal narratives, plays, a volume of poetry by veterans, and several novels. He likes to include one novel that has been published within a year or so of the course date, and he runs a biweekly film series, requiring students to see at least three films during the course (1989, 35).

Another approach is to design units and courses which combine the literature of the Vietnam War with literature from other wars. One focus might be on twentieth-century war literature. Such a course might include literature from World War I, World War II, and the Vietnam War (as well as the Korean War, if time permits). The literature might be dealt with chronologically, by theme, or through a combination of both. In this way students see that the literature of the Vietnam War is part of a literary heritage. More important, like some of the texts we already teach (*The Red Badge of Courage, A Farewell to Arms, All Quiet on the Western Front,* and *Catch-22* among them), these works demand that students think about what it really meant to live and fight in this war and compare the experience with that of past wars.

Carter (1989) suggests a similar approach in which a Vietnam War literature unit is part of a larger unit which would include other American and European war literature. The advantage to this approach is that students see how the literature of the Vietnam War relates to other American and European literature. Smagorinsky and Gevinson (1989) suggest a unit on "War and Peace" that contains classic war literature, as well as important Vietnam War literature, including Tim O'Brien's *Going after Cacciato,* and which might include films such as *Apocalypse Now, Coming Home, The Deer Hunter,* or *Platoon.* A unit with this kind of focus might also include literature dealing with the antiwar movement, including works such as Norman Mailer's *The Armies of the Night.*

Christie points out that the literature of the Vietnam War also raises provocative questions about gender and race. Increasingly, women are relating their own stories of the war. Linda Van Devanter's memoir, *Home before Morning* (1983), Keith Walker's oral history of women who served in Vietnam, *A Piece of My Heart* (1985), and Bobbie Ann Mason's novel *In Country* (1985) explore gender issues and the Vietnam experience. Racial issues are examined in a number of the works dealing with the Vietnam War. In particular, Wallace Terry's oral history of black Vietnam veterans, *Bloods* (1984), examines the black experience in the Vietnam War.

Works about the war also provide numerous opportunities to examine the nature and power of language. Christie points out that his students are fascinated by the distinctive language they encounter in the literature of the Vietnam War. Words and phrases like "frag," "grunt," "klick," "slick," "blown away," and "wasted," for instance, were part of the common vocabulary which is alien to most of the young people we teach. Christie points out that the euphemisms and acronyms of militarese, as well as the slogans of political propaganda and the colorful catchphrases of the counterculture and rock-and-roll, contributed to the deceptive and often dangerous "doublespeak" in which the war was discussed, or what Herr (1978) describes as "language fix and press relations" (43). One example Herr gives of this linguistic phenomenon involves a "tunnel rat" he interviewed on that day in 1968 when General Westmoreland made his famous "light at the end of the tunnel" plea for more troops. When Herr asked the soldier from the tunnel for his opinion, the soldier almost smiled and asked, "What does that asshole know about tunnels?" (49). Or, as Herr explains, after four months of "sweeping" through the "DMZ" in the fall of 1967, the Marines were officially "containing" at Con Thien, which really meant that they were "sitting there while the NVA killed them with artillery" (49). In addition, Anisfield (1988) argues that the language in these works is intensified beyond the colloquialisms contained in standard narratives and enables these writers to show the physical and psychic atmosphere of the war and gives them more dimensions through which to comment on the war. Gilman (1988) indicates that the special language of the literature of the Vietnam War is a key feature. He refers to it as "paradoxical paradigm of nomenclature" and argues that it works to produce a literature that is charged with particularity, intensity, brutality, and irony.

Teaching the literature and film of the Vietnam War offers numerous opportunities for integrating literature and writing with other curricular areas, particularly social studies. In fact, Wilcox notes that teaching the literature of the Vietnam War "is an opportunity to examine the historical origins, political and military confusions, and the social, economic, and spiritual costs of America's longest and most unpopular war" (1988, 40). Steven Cohen (1988), who teaches history at the Cambridge School of Weston in Massachusetts, describes a Vietnam War history course that sounds very much like a good Vietnam War literature course because it includes Graham Greene's *The Quiet American*, Philip Caputo's *A Rumor of War*, Michael Herr's *Dispatches*, James Webb's *Fields of Fire*, Jack Fuller's *Fragments*, and Bobbie Ann Mason's *In Country*. Goldstein (1989), who teaches an undergraduate Vietnam War history course, argues that including literary works and films in a Vietnam War history course is essential because the Vietnam War was fought and lost as much on the battlefield as it was on the printed page and on the television screen. Cussler (1987) describes how a unit on oral history in her high school communications class used the experiences of local veterans and others affected by the war to provide background on writing, history, and oral history techniques.

Finally, teaching the literature of the Vietnam War offers numerous opportunities to encourage student response to literature. Recent research on young adult reading preferences reveals that this literature has a strong impact on students. In the 1989 and 1990 International Reading Association's annual surveys of young adults' reading choices, three works of Vietnam War literature were preferred by readers in middle, junior high, and senior high schools: Bernard Edelman's *Dear America: Letters Home from Vietnam* (a 1989 choice) and Mary Downing Hahn's *December Stillness* and Walter Dean Myers's *Fallen Angels* (both 1990 choices).

Students' high level of involvement with this literature is evident in the classroom. Mandel (1988) notes that not only did she and her students learn and open up as a result of their discussions of *A Boat to Nowhere,* but while it was not her original intent to provide a therapeutic experience for her students, that is exactly what happened in an informal way. Oldham (1986), who concludes his course by having students do an oral history project on the Vietnam War, reports that his students almost always write more than the minimum, that the quality is often unusually good, and that their oral histories and other writings are remarkably introspective. Carter (1989 and 1991) also has her students study oral history interviews from the Vietnam War. She then has them interview veterans and transcribe the oral histories for a class collection. Carter reports that in an age when teenagers have little significant contact with adults, the impact of these interviews on her students has been nothing short of "electric."

My own experience is similar. I often have my students write personal responses to some of the literature and film and write at least one formal literary analysis of a major work. Their writing is almost always better than I think it will be. Why? Somehow I think that it is related to my earlier contention: The literature of the Vietnam War speaks directly to them in many ways, most of all through the "gut." As a result, their responses are written as much from the heart as from the head. Here is what some of my students had to say in response to some of the literature and film of the Vietnam War:

> After reading about what these boys had to live through [from Mark Baker's *Nam*], I learned something that I did not learn in history class. I learned what the Vietnam War was like from the eyes of the soldiers there—not as it was for the politicians safe in Washington, D.C.

The following responses were written by students after they viewed the film *Dear America: Letters Home from Vietnam:*

Student 1:

I recommend the movie to all people who have misconceptions of what that war was like and about the men and women who fought it. I assure them, they will leave the film with a tear in their eye and a desire to find a Vietnam veteran and hug him or her!

Student 2:

One startling factor of the film was in finding out that the people in America knew little or nothing about what the war was really like. In hearing that a mother sent her son "wing tips" [shoes] while he was in 'Nam, I wanted to slap her and tell her to wake up! This woman had to be really stupid or totally denying the truth to think her son could use wing tips in Vietnam.

Another student had this interesting response to *Dear America*:

The letter home that really struck me was the one by Raymond Griffiths. He writes to his friend how worried he is that he will lose his girlfriend. This reminded me of my boyfriend and I thought how romantic it would be if he went away to war and remembered me in the middle of all the fighting. But, as I was imagining this, Ray's picture appeared on the screen, and under it flashed the words, "Raymond Griffiths was killed a few weeks later on the Fourth of July. He was 19 years old, the average age of a combat soldier in Vietnam." As I read those lines a feeling of guilt came over me. How could I ever imagine (wish) or consider such a thing—wanting my boyfriend to go to war just so I could receive a romantic letter from him? I felt guilty as I imagined my boyfriend in war risking his life because I wanted a little romance.

For many students it was the novels that had the most impact on them. One student wrote the following response to *Fields of Fire*:

Fields of Fire was the most interesting, eye-opening novel I have ever read. It helped me understand what actually happened in Vietnam and helped me disregard my misconceptions I had had previously.

These responses are interesting for two reasons: first, these students clearly learned some important lessons about the war from studying the literature and films of the Vietnam War; yet, what each learned is as much, or perhaps more, a powerful affective response as it is intellectual. If one of our goals in teaching literature is that it will have a profound impact on students, that it will move them, that it will be more than an intellectual exercise they do in school, then these student responses stand as a testament to the potential impact the best literature and film of the Vietnam War can have on our students.

CRITICAL STUDIES OF VIETNAM WAR LITERATURE AND FILM

> "... I have read the literature. I've read these books because the war so changed the men and women who fought; it changed those who protested the war at home; it even changed those who tried to ignore what was happening to America. It changed us all. I've read these books to try to understand how and why."
>
> —C.D.B. Bryan, "Barely Suppressed Screams: Getting
> a Bead on Vietnam War Literature"

There is a substantial and growing body of fine Vietnam War literature that, until quite recently, has been perhaps the best-kept secret in the literary world. Hollywood, with its series of popular Vietnam War movies, including *Platoon, Full Metal Jacket,* and *Born on the Fourth of July,* has had a great deal to do with sparking interest in the Vietnam War, particularly with young people (Johannessen 1990). Wittman (1989) indicates that the one-time trickle of literature about the war has become a flood since the mid-1980s. Many bookstores now boast Vietnam sections.

While works dealing with the war have been written and published since the early days of America's involvement in Southeast Asia, why has this body of literature remained largely in the shadows? One reason, of course, is that until recently most of this literature has not been well-received by the critics and scholars. In addition, the publishing industry and even Hollywood, perhaps reflecting public interest, have only recently come to see the Vietnam War as worthy of serious consideration. For example, Naparsteck (1979) points out that the unpopularity of the war with publishers made it virtually impossible for writers to get manuscripts dealing with Vietnam published. Jervis Jurjevics, who worked in publishing for over fifteen years, admitted in 1985:

> We sat for years in editorial boards and marketing meetings turning down novel after novel. . . . For a period of time well into the 1970s, the Vietnam novel was really an obscenity. . . . Ironically some of the ones turned down went on ten years later to win first novel awards. (Lomperis 1987, 44)

Lomperis notes that Bill Ehrhart had to wait ten years for any of his poetry to be published, and Wallace Terry, author of *Bloods: An Oral History of the Vietnam War by Black Veterans,* was rejected by 120 publishers (1987, 43–44). It is no secret that it took nearly ten years for Oliver Stone to get anyone to back his screenplay for *Platoon.* Our national amnesia about the war, coupled with a chilly reception by publishers and Hollywood and an even chillier reception by critics and scholars, has kept the literature of the Vietnam War very much in the shadows.

However, there is now a considerable and rapidly growing body of critical studies on the literature and film of the Vietnam War. In a recent bibliography of critical works on Vietnam War literature, Wittman (1989) lists over 250 articles and book-length critical studies, over fifty dissertations and theses, nearly thirty bibliographies, and this is not counting the nearly sixty critical studies on Vietnam War films. An examination of a mere handful of these studies provides a strong rationale for teaching the literature and film of the Vietnam War, and suggests ways to approach teaching them. In general, the critical studies trace the major styles and themes and compare them with those of other wars. One conclusion that very quickly becomes apparent is that the literature and film of the Vietnam War, like the war itself, are both connected to and in many ways unique to the great tradition of American and war literature.

Thomas Myers's *Walking Point: American Narratives of Vietnam* (1988) is a particularly useful critical study because in it he shows how some of the best fiction and memoirs to come out of the war are indebted to Crane, Melville, and Cooper and how their work is as much a part of our national literature as the work of Heller, Mailer, Jones, and Hemingway. In addition, this study assesses the most important novels and personal memoirs written by Americans about the Vietnam War. Myers shows how unique aspects of the war demanded the revision of traditional modes of war writing or the discovery of new styles that would render the emotional and psychological center of a new national trauma.

Another important study is John Hellmann's *American Myth and the Legacy of Vietnam* (1989). Using American literature and film, especially works dealing with the Vietnam era, he traces the relationship of America's mythic heritage to its experience in Vietnam and shows how the Vietnam experience has severely called into question American myth. Philip D. Beidler's *American Literature and the Experience of Vietnam* (1982) is an important and useful survey of the literature of the Vietnam War. He relates Vietnam War literature to the process of cultural myth-making and examines major themes and styles. Beidler also discusses how the literature might be examined in terms of when it was written, 1958–70, 1970–75, 1975–present. Another important and useful work is Timothy J. Lomperis's *"Reading the Wind": The Literature of the Vietnam War—an Interpretive Critique* (1987). This study is the result of a conference held by the Asia Society in 1985 at which many of the major Vietnam writers spoke. The study examines the Vietnam novel and its role in American literature. Perhaps the most useful part of this work is John Clark Pratt's "Bibliographic Commentary: 'From the Fiction, Some Truths'" (117–54). Pratt places Vietnam novels within the framework of the history of the war.

From a teaching standpoint, William J. Searle's *Search and Clear: Critical Responses to Literature and Films of the Vietnam War* (1988) is the most useful critical work available. It is a collection of sixteen essays on Vietnam and its portrayal in literature and film. It contains essays that examine everything from major dramas to narrative style in novels, from the legacy of Joseph Conrad's *Heart of Darkness* in Vietnam War fiction, memoirs, and film to the use of language and how it conveys meaning, from how movies have dealt with the war to the war in personal narratives, from the adolescent experience in fiction and narratives to women involved in the war and their depiction in novels and personal narratives. Taken together, this collection indicates a wide variety of approaches that might be used in designing instruction on the literature and film of the Vietnam War. It also provides many insights into handling some of the unique aspects of the literature and film.

Jeffrey Walsh's *American War Literature: 1914 to Vietnam* (1982) presents an introduction to modern American war literature, and in the last chapter, notes the differences between the poetry, drama, and fiction of the Vietnam War and previous wars. Many will find C.D.B. Bryan's "Barely Suppressed Screams: Getting a Bead on Vietnam War Literature" (*Harper's*, June 1984) a very useful primer on Vietnam War literature. He explores the relationship between the literature of the Holocaust and that of the Vietnam War, and presents the archetypal Vietnam War story based on his analysis of major novels and memoirs. Terry Farish's "If You Knew Him, Please Write Me: Novels about the War in Vietnam" (*School Library Journal*, November 1988) is a brief but excellent analysis of how the war is portrayed in books for children and young adults. Finally, one of the most useful works I have found is Sandra M. Wittman's *Writing about*

Vietnam: A Bibliography of the Literature of the Vietnam Conflict (1989). This annotated bibliography is invaluable to anyone interested in gaining access to the vast body of literature generated in response to the Vietnam conflict. It cites over 1,700 works of fiction and nonfiction, as well as scholarly and reference works. Of particular value are the sections on novels, personal narratives and biographies (including oral histories), poetry, drama, short stories, anthologies, and literary criticism. As an added bonus, it even contains a section on published teaching materials.

These and other critical studies place Vietnam War literature in the great tradition of American and war literature and indicate the significant contribution it has made and continues to make to our national literature. The inescapable conclusion of the critical response to the literature and film of the Vietnam War is that if our goal is to help students understand themselves and the world they live in and to prepare them for the future, then we cannot ignore this important chapter of our literary heritage. We must find ways to incorporate it into the literature curriculum for all students. To do less, may be to doom our students to repeat the mistakes of the past.

OUT OF THE SHADOWS AND INTO THE CLASSROOM

> "There is a duty to look this war in the face and to look at it without vanity or ego or pretention or narrow idealogy."
>
> —Ward Just, "Vietnam: The Camera Lies"

One of the concerns that many teachers have about teaching the literature of the Vietnam War is that their own views on the war may get in the way of their teaching. Glassman (1988), who has taught courses and conducted workshops for teachers on the Vietnam War, says that the teachers he has worked with "repeatedly expressed concerns about personal bias and the danger of teaching only their own opinions." Starr (1988a) notes that teachers he has worked with fear that their biases will invalidate the learning experiences for their students.

One answer to this problem is that we *must* overcome teaching from narrow views of the war. Why? The consequences of teaching only one viewpoint and possibly invalidating the learning experiences for students are great. Our students may remain ignorant of the recent past; they may continue to view the war in terms of the dangerous misconceptions and distortions they came to us believing; they may learn little about this chapter of America's literary heritage;

they may not understand how the aftermath of the war continues to shape their lives and society; and they may not be prepared to make informed, intelligent decisions about the future. In fact, with their myths and media images of the war still intact, there does not seem to be much to prevent them from thinking that they can control and limit the effects of war, just as the Vietnam generation thought that it could.

However, knowing that we must be more objective in our teaching and actually being objective when we teach, particularly when we may have strong feelings about the subject, is much easier said than done. In the Introduction to his collection of critical essays on the literature and film of the Vietnam War, Searle (1988) argues that one way to get beyond our biases is to become familiar with some of the critical studies dealing with this literature. Knowing more about the literature is certainly an important first step, but it does not fully answer the question. In fact, Wilcox wonders:

> What pedagogical strategies can we teachers use to describe the war that divided our nation, destroyed a genera-tion's confidence in government, and left a legacy of distrust, self-doubt, guilt, and recrimination? How can we convey the horrors of a conflict that appears to defy accurate description? (1988, 39)

The solution to the problem, according to Wilcox, is to rely on teaching the literature of the war written by veterans and others involved in the war. He argues that it is "through these texts—painful, angry, poignant, almost unbearably honest at times—that students can begin to discover America's longest and most unpopu-lar war" (39). This solution also seems to be a step in the right direction, but it still does not provide a complete answer. It does not explain how to handle these texts in the classroom.

Glassman argues that the solution to the problem is to gain greater command of the facts. He maintains that teachers need to understand the facts that support their opinions about the war as well as those that challenge them. This may also be an important step, but it still does not provide a clear answer to how to go about teaching the literature of the Vietnam War.

My solution to this problem is that, in deciding both what we teach and how we teach it, we must adopt a teaching stance that will enable our students to discover for themselves the essential truth of the war. In describing her unit on Vietnam War literature, Carter explains that her goal "was not to spend a lot of time on the events of the war." Instead, she "wanted to help students realize, through literature and language, what the war in Vietnam was like and what its legacy has been for all of us" (1991, 292).

Oldham, a high school teacher and Vietnam veteran, offers another perspective on this issue. After teaching a course on the literature of the Vietnam War, he worried that his students were caught up in the same "John Wayneism" that characterized the early years of the war. He expressed concern that many of his students said they would allow themselves to be drafted during time of war, but in the end, he reminds himself that "[his] job as a teacher is to prepare [his] students to reach their own conclusions, not to force [his] upon them" (1986, 56). Like Carter, Oldham sees the importance of moving beyond his own views and adopting a teaching stance that encourages students "to reach their own conclusions" about the war.

In selecting materials it is certainly important to seek out those that will appeal to and be appropriate for our students, show them what the war was like, reveal what the legacies are, and reflect in some measure the best of the literature that is available. In addition, an attempt should be made to select materials that reflect a wide range of viewpoints and issues.

In teaching this literature, we need to design instruction so that students discover truths for themselves. This means students must have opportunities to express and debate their own views, interpretations, and conclusions. It means stepping back from the role of teacher as dispenser of knowledge and "right" answers and assuming a role of facilitator or coach who encourages students to discuss and debate with one another and arrive at their own conclusions and interpretations. It means avoiding teacher-to-student debates, which students often interpret to mean that their views are not acceptable and/or that they will be "graded down" if they disagree with the teacher. The following excerpt from a class discussion of the Walter Dean Myers novel *Fallen Angels* illustrates how one teacher maintained an objective stance and enabled students to come to understand an important passage in the novel:

> **Teacher:** What did Perry want to do when he graduated from high school?
>
> **Mark:** He wanted to go to college and be a writer like James Baldwin.
>
> **Teacher:** Why didn't he do that?

Lita: I thought it was because he had to make money to help his family out.

Teacher: Dan, you wanted to say something?

Dan: I think he was really stupid for going into the Army. I mean, he knew the war was going on. What did he think was going to happen to him if he went in the Army? And if he needs to help his family out, why doesn't he get a job. I mean, most jobs would pay more than he would make in the Army.

Teacher: Interesting. Do you all agree with that?

Marcia: I think Dan is wrong. Perry's family is poor. It looks like they may live in a ghetto or some place like that.

Dan: So what? They are poor and black. Didn't the guy listen to what was going on? People were protesting the war and pointing out how stupid it was and stuff.

Marcia: Wait a minute! I think the author wants us to see that for many blacks there weren't many options. Perry has to wear the same school clothes every day. And, it says, "How was I going to get the clothes for college? How was I going to get clothes for Kenny so he would stay in school?" I think this shows that for people like Perry, the Army was one of the few options they had. I think he knew about the protest against the war, but it is different when you are talking about survival.

Teacher: Hum. Dan, is there anything else you would like to add?

Dan: I guess Marcia is right. I mean, a lot of the protesters were college students. Perry is in a different situation.

Thus, the discussion begins with the teacher asking the class to consider why Perry decides to go into the military. As the discussion develops, one student interprets Perry's decision to go into the Army as evidence that he is not very smart. The teacher could easily have challenged Dan on his interpretation, which might have appeared to be a confrontation between the student and the teacher. Instead, the teacher asks the students if they all agree with Dan's analysis. Basing her comments on information from the text, Marcia responds with the argument that, war or no war, for the poor the military was one of the few economic options available. Dan responds by pointing out that it is hard for him to believe that Perry was unaware of the controversy over the war in Vietnam. Marcia counters by pointing to specific references in the text that illustrate the very difficult economic situation Perry's family was in and why the military was the only answer for Perry. Finally, the teacher maintains an objective stance by offering Dan a chance to react to Marcia. Dan, however, has been convinced by Marcia's argument. In this excerpt, the teacher maintains an objective stance throughout the discussion, asking questions and encouraging students to support their interpretations and challenge the views of others. In this way, the students themselves arrive at an interpretation of the text.

Maintaining this objective teaching stance also means creating instruction that will encourage students to think critically about what they are reading and providing opportunities for students to discuss and defend their viewpoints at length, orally and in writing. Finally, it means creating instruction that will involve students in problem-solving situations for which there are no transparent answers. In a very real sense, adopting this teaching stance will enable us to begin the process of healing the "wounds" of the war.

A classroom example may help illustrate these points. One of the activities in the practice section, "On Patrol #4: With the Enemy," has students examine two short stories that focus on what the war was like from the Viet Cong point of view: David Huddle's "The Interrogation of the Prisoner Bung by Mister Hawkins and Sergeant Tree" and Larry Rottmann's "Thi Bong Dzu." Some teachers might raise questions about teaching these stories because they deal primarily with the enemy. However, they provide a different look at the war, and the authors are able to point out aspects of the war that are often overlooked in other literature. My students are usually very interested in these stories. They seem to view reading them as a kind of behind-the-scenes look at life with the enemy.

After reading the stories, students answer a series of questions in small groups. The questions direct students to focus on how the Vietnamese view the Americans, aspects of Vietnamese culture, why they feel empathy for certain characters and not for others, and what the authors are saying about the Vietnam War. Once students have answered the questions in small groups, I lead a class discussion.

Students become engaged in this activity for a couple of important reasons. First, the stories are skillfully written. Students find themselves feeling empathy for the enemy soldiers and not for the Americans and South Vietnamese. They begin to see why the South Vietnamese were so inept and corrupt and why the Viet Cong were so intractable. Students also become engaged because there is no obvious answer in terms of what the authors are saying about the war. Some interpret both authors as being antiwar, while others focus on how cultural differences contributed to misunderstandings between Americans and Vietnamese or how ridiculous Americans looked in their reliance upon technology.

In the small-group and whole-class discussions, students must "dig" to arrive at meaning and often must battle with their own stereotyped views of the enemy. Inevitably, controversy arises in the discussions. Students begin to look for evidence from the text because they want to explain and defend their positions. From their work in small groups, students arrive at an interpretation and are less likely to accept uncritically any answer that is given.

In addition, the small-group work helps students to search independently because they cannot look to the teacher for constant confirmation of the "correct" answer. The activity is designed so that the teacher's role is to coach or facilitate the students in their search for meaning. One of the suggested follow-up activities has students examine a third story dealing with the enemy and write an interpretation of it. This step is important in terms of the teaching stance I have discussed. The small-group and whole-class discussions of the two stories have given students practice in critical thinking and in interpreting this literature in a problem-solving situation. Now, students have a similar problem, but one that they must solve on their own. The teacher's role is not to "tell" students the literary techniques used or the author's meaning, but rather to move students toward being independent of the teacher, to enable students to be independent thinkers and readers.

This activity illustrates the kind of thinking behind most of the activities in the practice section, which involve students in problem-solving situations that require critical thinking, promote student-to-student interaction, encourage students to arrive at their own interpretations and conclusions, and provide opportunities for students to elaborate on and defend their interpretations. The teacher is the coach who orchestrates the learning experience so that students make their own discoveries and arrive at their own conclusions and insights. The teaching stance I am suggesting follows the recommendations of the English Coalition Conference (Lloyd-Jones and Lunsford, 1989).

In addition to addressing the issue of teaching stance, the practice section attempts to address many other concerns teachers have about teaching Vietnam War literature and to overcome some of the obstacles one might encounter in trying to teach it. The practice section also attempts to bring together and put into practice current knowledge from critical theory and research on Vietnam War literature and film and the most promising teaching practice from published and unpublished sources. The sample activities and assignments are designed to illustrate a range of approaches, as well as to show how to present a wide range of the available literature and film.

Following the practice section is a list of "Selected and Annotated Resources for Classroom Use." The list contains recommended nonfiction for teachers who want to learn more about the war before attempting to teach it. In addition, the list includes titles of some of the best available literature dealing with the Vietnam War for use in elementary, secondary, and undergraduate classrooms. Many of the titles have been or are currently being used by classroom teachers.

Each title includes an annotation which briefly describes the content of the work and gives an indication of difficulty or appropriateness for particular students. In addition, if I and/or others have had success in the classroom with a work, I indicate that the work is highly recommended for use in the classroom.

USING THE PRACTICE SECTION

The practice section contains numerous sample activities for teaching the literature of the Vietnam War. I have included a variety of approaches and activities for teaching all types of Vietnam War literature. There are activities for introducing students to individual works or units and for doing history and background research and reports on the war. In addition, there are activities that encourage students to examine music, art, and photography dealing with the war. I have included activities for teaching poetry, short stories, drama and film, personal narratives, and novels.

The activities are meant to serve as models for designing instruction. They also serve other important purposes. First, they seem to me to be consistent with the elements of the teaching stance I outlined above. In addition, they all seem to be activities which will help students understand the war and the literature of the war. Finally, the activities are ones which, as Christie (1989) says, will help "students see themselves and their world more clearly."

The activities can be used in different ways. Many of the activities might be used individually or together with particular works, or they might be put together to form various units and courses. One option is to follow one of the unit or course outlines presented above using various suggested works and activities from the practice section. In addition, the practice section contains suggestions for other possible units and courses. It is also possible to design original units or courses using various works and activities in the practice section.

Most of the activities are designed for secondary students with the idea that elementary and college teachers can modify them or design similar activities for their students. I have included suggestions for follow-up activities for writing or speaking, as well as suggestions for ways to modify activities. While many of the activities are designed to accompany specific works of literature, I try to indicate alternative works whenever possible. In addition, there are suggestions given for how activities and specific works might be used in conjunction with other works and activities. Finally, the discussion of many of the activities also includes a reference to one or more student activity sheets in the appendix that may be copied for classroom use.

Some exciting and challenging sequences, units, and courses might be arranged using various activities and suggested works in the practice section. For example, if time is a major problem or if the teacher wants to try a modest unit, then one possible three-to-four week unit might include the following:

> **First Contact #1:** Vietnam War Opinionnaire (introductory activity)
>
> **Burning Tracers:** Teaching Poetry
>
> **On Patrol #1:** Choices (short stories)
>
> **On Patrol #3:** Vietnam Lexicon (short story)
>
> **"Old Kids" #1:** The Adolescent Experience (personal narrative)

This unit begins with an introductory activity that is designed to elicit students' opinions and knowledge and to introduce some key concepts on which the literature will focus. It is designed to enhance purposeful reading and increase comprehension once they begin reading. Students respond to a list of statements about patriotism, ethical values, and war. They are asked to agree or disagree with statements such as "Rambo is a good image for Americans to have of the Vietnam veteran: he represents all that America stands for and the American soldier in war," "Ask not what your country can do for you—ask what you can do for your country," or "People should never compromise their ideals or beliefs." In a class discussion of students' responses, they must explain and defend their opinions to their peers. Some students are surprised to discover that some of their peers are not so willing to accept Rambo as a desirable or realistic image of the soldiers who fought in

Vietnam. In later discussions of poetry, short stories, and personal narratives, the teacher can refer to the opinionnaire and ask students whether they think individual authors would agree or disagree with certain statements on the opinionnaire. At this point, students may begin to refine their own initial ideas as they take into account how the literature treats these ideas, which often challenge the stereo-types and myths students have acquired through the various media.

The introductory activity is followed by a sequence of three activities in which students examine several poems by Vietnam veterans. The poems introduce important themes and issues such as the horror of combat in Vietnam and the homecoming of veterans. In addition, the activities encourage students to examine these themes and how these poets achieve meaning in their poems. The first activity asks students to examine a single poem and provides key questions to guide reading. This is followed by a teacher-led discussion of the poem. Students next examine several poems in small groups, and then join in a class discussion of students' findings. Finally, students are asked to examine a poem on their own and write a brief composition explaining what the poet is saying about the Vietnam War and how the poem achieves meaning.

In the next activity, "On Patrol #1: Choices," students examine two short stories that focus on one inevitable outcome of the war in Vietnam—brutality—and a major literary technique used by many Vietnam War writers to convey meaning—irony. The stories also directly challenge the media-molded myths and images that students have regarding Hollywood's version of the war. Students examine the stories in small groups, and after a class discussion of their findings, students read and write about a third story that relies on irony to convey meaning.

In "On Patrol #3: Vietnam Lexicon," students examine a story that uses the language of the war. As part of the activity, students are introduced to what the language of the war is. Then, using what they have learned about the Vietnam lexicon, they examine the story and determine what the author is saying about the war through the use of this language.

In the final activity of this modest unit, students read a personal narrative which focuses on the adolescent experience of coming of age using Lawson's (1988) conception of the structural and thematic elements of these works. The model narrative is Mark Baker's oral history *Nam*, but any one of a number of excellent personal narratives might be used in its place.

More ambitious units might be put together using this same basic structure. To add a novel, the teacher might follow the suggestions in "Lessons and Legacies #1: The Vietnam Experience." This activity shows how to use Lawson's "Old Kids" approach to teach a Vietnam War novel. If the teacher wants to examine the effects of the war on veterans and the children of Vietnam veterans, then "Lessons and Legacies #2: The Next Generation" illustrates how to teach Mason's novel *In Country*. Another possibility for teaching a novel is contained in the final series of five activities, "'Some Truths': Character Analysis in a Novel." This sequence of activities illustrates how to teach a novel by focusing on how the main characters change as a result of their experiences in Vietnam. It culminates with students writing an analysis of one of the main characters. These activities also follow Lawson's "Old Kids" approach and therefore show one way to link personal narratives with novels. "Lessons and Legacies #3: Graphic Presentation" is an unusual activity that is designed to encourage students to use visual and linguistic imagery to express the themes, characters, and structure of a novel they study.

There are a number of other possibilities for teaching personal narratives. For example, "'Old Kids' #2: Independent Reading" illustrates one way to teach personal narratives using an independent reading format. "'Old Kids' #3: Guest Speakers" shows how to use oral histories for study and as models for interviewing and writing about Vietnam veterans and others who participated in the war. "'Old Kids' #4: Living History" illustrates how to have students collect their own oral histories of the Vietnam War. "'Old Kids' #5: Homefront U.S.A." shows how to use personal narratives and other nonfiction documents to teach students about the war at home and some of the legacies of the war.

For teachers who want to include drama and film in their instruction, the practice section offers four possibilities. "Acts of War #1: Drama" describes an activity for teaching Ronald Ribman's television drama "The Final War of Ollie Winter." The play offers opportunities for studying the Vietnamese people and the difficulties black Americans faced in the military during the Vietnam War. "Acts of War #2: A Documentary Film: Letters from the Combat Zone" describes one approach to teaching a documentary film on the Vietnam War. The model activity focuses on *Dear America: Letters Home from Vietnam* and how to use this powerful film to help students understand the Vietnam War. The activity also provides opportunities for sharpening analytical skills and for personal writing on the film. "Acts of War #3: A Documentary Film: Frontline America" shows how to use one of the many documentary films dealing with the war at home. The model activity uses the highly acclaimed *Vietnam: The War at Home* to help students understand the impact of the war on the home front. Teachers who want to teach one of the excellent feature-length films dealing with the Vietnam War should consider "Acts of War #4: A Feature-Length Film." Using Stanley Kubrick's *Full Metal Jacket* as a model, the activity illustrates one approach to teaching one of the major motion pictures to come out of the war.

There are three additional activities for short stories. Many students have difficulty understanding exactly who the enemy was in Vietnam. "On Patrol #4: With the Enemy" shows how to use two short stories that focus on Viet Cong soldiers to help students understand a bit about the Vietnamese, the enemy, and the cultural gap that may have at least contributed to our inability to win the war. "On Patrol #2: 'Night March'" provides an opportunity for students to examine an important theme in much of the literature of the war, one which has provided a basis for some of the experimental fiction that has been written. Using Tim O'Brien's short story "Night March," students examine the role of fear and imagination and how these work on a young soldier during his first day in Vietnam. "On Patrol #5: The War at Home" offers another opportunity for students to examine the impact of the war on the home front. This activity uses a number of short stories dealing with the war at home. Students study the effects of the war on individuals opposed to the war and some of the legacies of the war.

There are also activities in which students do research on the war. In "Operation Search #1: History and Background," students conduct library research on a Vietnam-related topic of their choice and report their findings to the class. Students explore diverse topics such as French colonialism in Vietnam, the antiwar movement in the U.S., the Tet Offensive of 1968, the draft, agent orange, and the Vietnamese Boat People. "Operation Search #2: Music, Art, and Photography" has students research and share how the war has been portrayed in the arts.

Finally, there are three additional introductory activities that might be used in different ways to motivate and prepare students for reading. "First Contact #2: Patriotism, Protest, and War Opinionnaire" is similar to the "Vietnam War Opinionnaire" described above, but deals with more issues and is best suited as an introduction to themes and issues in longer units and courses. It attempts, among other things, to link a number of themes and concepts in Vietnam War literature with the war literature from other wars. "First Contact #3: Heroism Scenarios" is an activity that is designed to help students deal with the concept of courage and how it is presented in the literature. Finally, "First Contact #4: Mines and Booby Traps Simulation" is a classroom simulation activity that is designed to give students a feel for what it was like to be a soldier and walk the trails in the bush of Vietnam. It gives students a taste of what they will encounter in their reading.

The activities explained in the practice section can be combined to create a variety of challenging and interesting sequences, units, and courses. As presented, they are intended to serve as models for activity design that teachers can follow in creating instruction to meet the needs and interests of their own students. I present the activities as they would be used with specific literary works in order to illustrate clearly the procedures and classroom dynamics. It is my hope that the activities and suggested works meet the goals Endres calls for in arguing for teaching Vietnam War literature:

> I believe that teaching the American literature of the Vietnam War serves two purposes. Students will see an abstract historical event in human terms. It allows students to see literature as a means for understanding, or at least viewing, life. The teacher can introduce thinking and reasoning skills, which . . . may permit future decisions to be made more carefully. (1984, 28)

2 Practice

"I think that Vietnam was what we had instead of happy childhoods."

—Michael Herr, *Dispatches*

ACTIVITIES FOR TEACHING VIETNAM WAR LITERATURE

First Contact: Introductory Activities

Students' lack of knowledge about the war presents a difficult problem for teachers who want to teach the literature and film of the Vietnam War: How to begin? Although it will be helpful to provide historical background and perhaps a bit of geography, as well as some information about the authors or filmmakers, this will probably not be enough for most students. The problem is that, besides knowing little historical background, most students lack a context or connection between their own lives and the literature they are about to study. One way to overcome this problem is through introductory activities. According to Smagorinsky and Gevinson (1989); Smagorinsky, McCann, and Kern (1987); Kahn, Walter, and Johannessen (1984); and Johannessen, Kahn, and Walter (1984), introductory activities are one way to help prepare students for some of the themes or concepts that they will be studying in a particular work or unit, help them with difficulties they are likely to confront in reading or interpreting, and interest or engage them in the work or unit they are about to study. In other words, introductory activities help provide a context or connection between students' lives and the literature they are studying, and also help to overcome some of the misconceptions they have about the war. I have included three types of introductory activities that seem to work well with a variety of literature and film of the Vietnam War: the opinionnaire, scenarios, and the simulation.

First Contact #1: Vietnam War Opinionnaire

The opinionnaire is based on a simple idea: Students have opinions about various subjects. The opinionnaire uses those opinions to create interest in a work of literature and helps with problems students will encounter in trying to interpret themes and characters.

In addition, this type of activity is designed to foster what Rosenblatt calls "fruitful . . . transactions between individual readers and individual literary works" (1968, 26–27).

"Vietnam War Opinionnaire" (see appendix, p. 145), is adapted from Johannessen (1989 and 1990), and I have used it, or variations of it, with a number of different literary works and films and as an introductory activity for a unit on Vietnam War literature and film. It is easily adaptable to a particular work or works that focus on the Vietnam War. Specifically, I have used it to introduce Tim O'Brien's "Centurion," from *If I Die in a Combat Zone;* Robin Moore's "We Have Met the Enemy," from *Combat Pay;* and Wayne Karlin's "Extract," from *Free Fire Zone: Short Stories by Vietnam Veterans.* In addition, I have used a variation of this opinionnaire to introduce a Vietnam War literature and film unit that included the above short stories, Mark Baker's oral history *Nam,* various poems, Webb's novel *Fields of Fire,* the documentary films *Dear America: Letters Home from Vietnam* and *Vietnam: The War at Home,* and Oliver Stone's *Platoon* (and most recently Stanley Kubrick's *Full Metal Jacket* instead of *Platoon*).

The first step in using the opinionnaire is to distribute it to the class, perhaps the day before it is going to begin a work. After students have responded to all the statements, I compile the results on the board. Then, beginning with the statements with which there is the most disagreement, I lead a class discussion that focuses on students' responses to each statement. I encourage students to explain the reasoning behind their responses and to debate differing opinions. For example, when a student agrees with statement 8, I encourage him or her to explain why. The response is usually something like "Americans have always responded when the nation has gone to war." Others often respond with "Anyone who believes that has watched too many old World War II movies!" I encourage other students to explain and argue their responses, but I also provide synthesis and direction as the need arises. Since the statements on the opinionnaire require students to take a stand, a lively discussion invariably ensues.

One purpose of the opinionnaire and follow-up discussion is to create interest in the characters and issues in the literature they are about to read. Statements 12 and 13, for example, relate to one aspect of the problem faced by the narrator of O'Brien's "Centurion," an issue that is common in much of the literature dealing with the Vietnam War. The officers in his unit randomly pull three old men out of a hut, tie them up, gag them, and then tie them to saplings in the center of the unit's perimeter, using the logic that the enemy guerrillas will not attack that night because they have taken their fathers prisoner. The narrator feels compassion for the old men. He thinks they may be innocent and knows that in the morning they will be tortured for information about the enemy. Yet he does almost nothing to help them. He seems to be unable to do anything significant about the brutality of the incident, accepting it as the price for survival in a crazy war.

Student responses to the statements on the opinionnaire that relate to this issue usually indicate that many of them believe that a person can do the right thing, not harm innocent civilians, and still survive in war. O'Brien and other authors and filmmakers suggest that in the Vietnam War the issue was not quite so black and white. Often, morality and compassion for innocent civilians take a back seat when survival is at stake. Through the class discussion of the opinionnaire, students begin to question some of their initial responses and are motivated to find out how characters will deal with these issues in the literature.

This activity also provides a framework or context that will help students understand what the authors or filmmakers want readers to understand about the Vietnam War. Many students have an oversimplified good-guys-against-the-bad-guys image of the war. In the discussion of the opinionnaire, students are often surprised to discover that some of their peers do not find the Rambo image accurate or desirable. In addition, in discussing the statements, at least one student inevitably notices that some of them are in quotes and wonders who said them. If no one in the class knows who said statement 6, for example, I reveal that it was made by President John F. Kennedy. As we discuss what he meant by his statement, I point out that this is a statement that often appears in the literature of the Vietnam War (for example, Ron Kovic's *Born on the Fourth of July* and Philip Caputo's *A Rumor of War*) and that as they read the literature they should look carefully at the impact Kennedy's statement had on various characters. Another quotation, statement 10, was made by Douglas MacArthur, one of America's greatest generals. Students are often very surprised by his quote, and as we discuss why MacArthur might have made such a statement and how it stands in striking contrast to Kennedy's patriotic call, students begin to realize that war is not as romantic as the images and myths of Hollywood's version of the Vietnam War. These and other questions on the opinionnaire help students construct a framework or context that will better enable them to understand the literature.

Once we have discussed most or all of the statements on the opinionnaire, I point out that the statements deal with problems and issues the characters face in the literature, and that they should keep them in mind as they read. In subsequent discussions and activities, I often refer to how students responded to statements on the opinionnaire and compare their responses to what they actually find in their reading or viewing. This activity serves as an important first step in closing the gap between students' experiences and the experience of a literary work.

First Contact #2: Patriotism, Protest, and War Opinionnaire

For a war-and-peace or war unit that would include Vietnam War literature, as well as literature from other wars, I would suggest the "Patriotism, Protest, and War Opinionnaire" (see appendix, p. 147). This particular opinionnaire was designed for a war unit that has included, at different times, Stephen Crane's *The Red Badge of Courage* and "The Upturned Face," Ernest Hemingway's *A Farewell to Arms,* Nelson Algren's "No Man's Laughter," Kurt Vonnegut's *Slaughterhouse Five,* Tim O'Brien's *If I Die in a Combat Zone* (or Philip Caputo's *A Rumor of War*), the PBS series "Vietnam: A History," and poetry from World Wars I and II and the Vietnam War. However, any number of important works might be included in a unit focusing on war literature or war and peace. This opinionnaire is adapted from Kahn, Walter, and Johannessen (1984) and Johannessen (1989).

This opinionnaire differs somewhat from the "Vietnam War Opinionnaire" in that it is designed to establish a context in terms of themes or issues as they are developed historically in war literature or as they are developed in a number of works. For example, the issue of courage is important in *The Red Badge of Courage, A Farewell to Arms,* and *If I Die in a Combat Zone.* In fact, both Hemingway and O'Brien use Shakespeare's idea, statement 1, in dealing with the issue. Hemingway ultimately rejects Shakespeare's concept of courage and establishes his own, centering on the idea of grace under pressure. O'Brien comes to Vietnam regarding Frederic Henry as one of his heroes, but struggles with Hemingway's definition, and eventually focuses on Frederic and Catherine's discussion of a baseball player who is a .230 hitter and knows he is no better. With this as his starting point, he finally decides on statement 7 as his definition of courage. Discussing these various definitions of courage prior to having students read these works will help them make connections when they encounter the theme in one or more works.

In addition, the statements on the opinionnaire are designed to help establish the context for some of the differences between America's previous war literature and the literature of the Vietnam War. For example, statement 15, which is in quotes, was made by a friend of mine with whom I joined the Marines in 1964. In 1968, a few months after I got back from Vietnam, my mother sent me a newspaper article about my friend. He had served with the 3rd Marines in Vietnam and had been awarded a Purple Heart and a Bronze Star for Heroism. When he returned home at the end of his tour, he found that his parents were giving him a party and had invited his family and friends. Cliff got out of the car and, without a word, limped to the front porch amid cheers and greetings and tore up the sign his little sister had made which proclaimed him a hero, and sounding like a line out of Michael Herr's *Dispatches*, scolded her by saying, "The only heroes in war are the dead ones." And the party was over.

His statement suggests many of the themes that emerge from Vietnam War literature: the issue of loss of innocence, the devastating physical and psychological tolls of the war on those who served, the devastating effects of the war on the home front, the questioning of traditional values, the search or quest for America, and echoes of the strong bond of brotherhood forged under fire (Johannessen 1989, 5–6). This is not to suggest that these themes are not in literature from other wars; rather, they take on new meaning in the literature of the Vietnam War. The activity helps establish a context that will enable students to understand these differences.

Another way that this activity works is that, in marking their answers, students, without realizing it, often contradict themselves. For example, some students agree with statements 2 and 13. As the class discussion develops, however, students realize (on their own or as a result of their peers pointing it out) that they have a contradiction in thought. It is not uncommon for one student to ask another, "How can you say it is never right to kill another person when you just got through saying that soldiers who refuse to fight should be shot as traitors?" In this way the discussion helps students sort out and clarify their thinking concerning the complex issues involved in war. They are, thus, better prepared for these issues when they encounter them in the literature.

The procedures for handling this opinionnaire in the classroom are essentially the same as those for the "Vietnam War Opinionnaire." However, an interesting variation is to have small groups of students discuss each statement before the whole class discussion. As a follow-up writing assignment, you might have students write a brief composition explaining why they agree or disagree with one or more of the statements on the opinionnaire. Once students have read some of the literature, another possibility is to have students write a composition explaining why the author or a character in a work would agree or disagree with one or more statements on the opinionnaire, giving evidence from the text to support their viewpoints. Another possible follow-up writing assignment is to have students select one of the statements and write an essay demonstrating, through reference to two or more works they have studied, whether these authors would agree or disagree with the selected statement.

First Contact #3: Heroism Scenarios

Scenarios are another method for introducing a literary work. They present everyday situations that involve a key concept critical for understanding a text. Providing everyday situations in the activity enables students to make connections between their own experiences and the specific world of the literary work. In addition, scenario-based activities attempt to spark interest in the subsequent text. The "Heroism: What Is a Heroic Act?" scenario-based activity (see appendix, p. 149) is adapted from one originally developed by Johannessen, Kahn, and Walter (1984) for a unit on the hero in literature.

The warrior-hero is one of the oldest figures portrayed in myth and history, with examples ranging from Achilles to the archetypal Rambo. Warrior-heroes are classically defined as persons who, tested by some type of war, demonstrate acts of heroism. However, like my Marine friend, who says that "The only heroes are the dead ones," many of the authors and filmmakers of Vietnam War literature and film found the classic definition of the warrior-hero inadequate. For example, in Ron Kovic's *Born on the Fourth of July* (both the memoir and Oliver Stone's film version), Ron fits the traditional warrior-hero model both as a high school athlete and as a Marine, but when he is in the VA hospital, and later as a political and antiwar activist, Ron becomes anything but the traditional warrior-hero. Many students, who come to the literature with their conventional myths and images, find it very difficult to accept the kind of hero presented in this type of literature and film.

The "Heroism: What Is a Heroic Act?" scenarios get students to do some serious thinking about the characteristics of or criteria for a heroic act and to confront viewpoints that may differ from their own before reading a work which deals with this concept.

To begin the activity have students individually fill out the "Heroism: What Is a Heroic Act?" activity sheet. After students have completed their individual rankings, they should be divided into small groups of three to five students. With other group members they try to reach a consensus. This is not easy since there is no one obviously best system of ranking. As students try to convince other group members that they are "right," they must elaborate the reasons for their choices. In deciding why, for instance, A is more or less heroic than B, students discover characteristics they think an action must have to be heroic and criteria that can be used to judge whether one action is more or less heroic than another. After the small groups complete their discussions, have the groups present their rankings to the whole class. At this point the debate begins again as groups defend their rankings. As the debate continues, lead students to a discussion of the qualities or criteria for deciding if an action is heroic. As students generate ideas, such as there must be a real danger or serious consequences and a willingness to sacrifice for others, list these on the board and have students copy them for future reference.

Students can apply these criteria as they read the literature and determine where within these rankings a particular character would fall. By examining these scenarios before they begin reading, students not only gain interest in the warrior-hero concept but also develop a more sophisticated understanding of the hero as they analyze the literature. In other words, this kind of activity may result in more purposeful reading when students begin a work such as *Born on the Fourth of July,* Jack Fuller's *Fragments,* Tim O'Brien's *If I Die in a Combat Zone* or *Going after Cacciato,* James Webb's *Fields of Fire,* or Lynda Van Devanter's *Home before Morning.* Students have something to look for—the attitudes, behavior, motivation, and actions of characters presented in the literature.

As a follow-up discussion or writing activity, students might rank the same scenarios as they think a particular author or character would rank them, and defend their choices with evidence from the literary work.

First Contact #4: Mines and Booby Traps Simulation

Another way to introduce a number of works of the Vietnam War is through a role-playing/simulation activity. The idea behind a simulation is the construction of an environment which requires the participants to take action and make decisions as if they are actually operating in the real environment. Smagorinsky, McCann, and Kern argue that such activities, when used prior to reading, enable students to grapple with concepts they will encounter in the reading and thereby improve students' comprehension of the material when they read it (1987, 7).

The following simulation, "Mines and Booby Traps," is adapted from Carter (1989 and 1991) and is designed to help students deal with some concepts that are key to understanding a number of works dealing with the Vietnam War. It is important to remember that mines and booby traps were a constant danger for soldiers in the war. This danger, the fear that it produced on the part of soldiers, and the cumulative effects of constantly taking casualties in this manner is a common thread running through many works. In addition, another related key concept that students need to understand is the degree to which soldiers in small units, fire teams, squads, platoons, and companies, depended on one another for survival. In works such as *Fields of Fire, Platoon, A Rumor of War,* and Tim O'Brien's works, we see the interplay of these issues. For example, in *Fields of Fire,* Lieutenant Hodges's constant frustration with taking casualties from mines, booby traps, and snipers contributes to his change in attitude toward the war. He came to the war as a young, gung-ho officer, but eventually concludes that the only true measure of success is how many of his men he brings back alive after each patrol.

This simulation requires a bit of preparation and planning. You will need to darken the classroom or a room where you can set up the minefield and booby traps. I darken the windows and set up coffee cans with black thread connecting them (using masking tape to attach the thread) across various parts of the room. I arrange the chairs in a labyrinth of trails and set the connected coffee cans at various levels and positions across the trails, some spread across the trails at ankle level, others at chest level, and still others at various angles. I leave one trail free of mines and booby traps, while another contains one or two, and two others have them every four or five feet. I also like to place a few interesting-looking articles (connected to coffee cans with black thread) on or near trails that students might see and pick up in the same way that many soldiers picked up interesting-looking items, only to discover that they were booby-trapped. Virtually any unusual or curious items that will likely attract students' attention will work, such as old canteens, articles of clothing, jewelry, old records, or just plain junk from the basement or garage. You will likely need a number of coffee cans and other items in order to set up enough mines and booby traps to make the problem challenging. The result of all this is that when students try to cross the room, most of them encounter a maze of mines and booby traps which, when knocked over, crash with a loud noise on the linoleum floor.

The next step is to divide the class into "squads" of four or five students whose task is to make it from one end of the room to another without tripping a mine or booby trap. After assigning the squads, I have each squad pick a squad leader, point man (to lead the patrol), radioman (who must carry a pack weighing about twenty pounds), and machine gunner (who must carry a rather heavy and awkward four-foot board). I then bring students into the room in squads and tell them that they must make it from one end of the room to the other without tripping any mines or booby traps. If they do hit a mine or booby trap, they have killed their squad.

Usually, about half the squads make it through. Some students ask if it is okay if they crawl, and actually do crawl across the room. Usually, at least one curious individual blows up his or her squad because he or she wants a closer look at those interesting-looking objects. Two or three squads pick the right trail and nothing happens. Another two or three pick the heavily mined and booby-trapped trail and do not make it. Other squads get nearly to the end, stop being so careful, and hit an angled mine stretched across a portion of the trail. In this activity students get a glimpse of the real terror of combat. This activity helps prepare them for the reality of Vietnam that they will encounter in the literature.

Once all students have gone through the simulation, the next step is to lead a class discussion of what they experienced. I use the following questions as a guide:

1. How did you decide who would play which role? Were your decisions right? Were they important? Why or why not?

2. Why did you pick the route you decided to take? Was it a wise decision? Why or why not? Was it a lucky decision? Why or why not?

3. Was teamwork important in your squad? Why or why not?

4. What makes a good leader in this situation? A good point man? A good radioman? A good machine gunner?

5. How did you feel as you went through the simulation?

6. What have you learned about the conditions of war in Vietnam from this activity?

As students discuss these questions, they begin to realize what it was like for soldiers in Vietnam. They talk about being cautious, a little scared that they or someone in their squad would set off a mine or booby trap, and the importance of communication within the squad. An alternative to the class discussion is to have students write a composition answering the above questions, and then have them share and discuss their responses. One of Carter's students had the following interesting response to going through a similar simulation: "The minefield . . . really made you put yourself in those men's shoes. You could understand what was really going on in their minds. I'm sure they must have been terrified all the time. And you really have to rely on all the other people to do their job, or your own life could be at stake . . ." (1989). As this response suggests, after doing this activity, students are prepared for dealing with the issues and characters they will encounter in the literature because they will be able to associate them with experiences and perceptions of their own that they have already explored.

Operation Search: Researching the War

A few years ago, I was sitting in the faculty lounge listening to a group of colleagues complain that they were tired of getting research papers on the same old topics and that they could not think of any interesting new topics for their junior American literature and American history students. They were particularly interested in controversial topics that would require their students to take a stand on issues. Finally, someone in the group turned to me and asked if I was having the same problem.

"No," I said. All eyes in the lounge turned to me. "I'm having my students do research on the Vietnam War."

That was the first year I had had my students do research on issues related to the Vietnam War, and while the results were far from perfect and I was already thinking about changes for the following year, I was fairly pleased.

This incident highlights an important point about the Vietnam War. It is a mistake to think that because the war is over, so are the issues related to the war. In fact, Goodman (1990) suggests that some of the really important questions about the Vietnam War have not as yet been asked, and he argues that "... the historical problem students need to consider above all is how long the aftermath of the Vietnam War will continue to shape their lives and society" (A36). Goodman provides a strong argument for teaching the Vietnam War and indicates why teachers should have their students do library research on the war: it is one way to help our students understand how the war affects them and the society in which they live. The activities that follow illustrate different ways the teacher can set up instruction that involves library research on the Vietnam War to achieve different instructional purposes.

Operation Search #1: History and Background

Christie points out that for this generation of students "... the Vietnam War might as well be the Peloponnesian War for all they know" (1989, 35). In fact, what little they do know is often inaccurate and distorted. If students are going to understand the literature and film of the Vietnam War, they will need to have some understanding of the historical context of the war, the people of Vietnam and Southeast Asia, and the geography of the region. In much of the literature, these elements are important to understanding plot, themes, and characters.

This activity is one way to help students learn some history and background on the war that will help them as they read the literature. The idea here is that instead of the teacher doing all the research on the history and background of the war and then presenting it to the class, the students do research on limited topics and report to the class on their findings. Before giving out the assignment (see appendix, p. 151), the teacher may want to check with the school and/or local library to make sure that they have materials on all of these topics, and then eliminate any topics that may be a problem. This list of topics is not meant to be exhaustive. Other topics are certainly possible depending on the ability and age of students and the availability of materials.

Once I have presented the assignment, I divide the class into small groups of three or four students. I then give the groups some time to look over, discuss, and pick a topic that interests them. However, no two groups may do the same topic. Another possibility is to put students into small groups based on the topics they have chosen. If the library has enough materials, it is certainly possible to have students research topics in pairs or on their own. However, I have found that having students research, plan, and give presentations in small groups is generally more effective. Students are not overwhelmed by the library research, have more fun doing the project, and do a better job.

I emphasize the fact that once they have done their research, they should divide the information they have gathered so that each person has a part in the oral presentation. Also, I tell them that each group is required to make at least one poster that will help illustrate the ideas, facts, and/or information that they present. I show samples of posters from previous years which contain photographs and drawings with accompanying captions. Usually, I set aside two class periods (and sometimes more depending on the age and ability level of students) for library research and planning of presentations. For younger and less able students, I would suggest limiting the time for oral presentations from ten to fifteen minutes. Time limits for older students might be twenty to thirty minutes. I also tell students that I will be evaluating their oral presentations on the following criteria: (1) the quality and thoroughness of content; (2) the quality and effectiveness of visual aids; and (3) the quality and effectiveness of the speakers. With younger and less able students who may have less experience with such projects, I usually research, plan, and do a presentation myself to provide a model of the process.

Excitement begins to build as students research and report on their topics. They are surprised to discover that there are so many issues involved in the war. More important, they begin to understand the historical context of the war and are better prepared for dealing with the literature. One natural follow-up activity is to have students apply what they have learned in their research and from other reports to the works they are studying. The teacher might ask students in discussions or in writing how specific topics apply to the works being studied. However, I have found that students themselves are quick to point out how some of the topics apply to the works the class is studying.

Operation Search #2: Music, Art, and Photography

Wade DallaGrana (1988), a high school social studies teacher, begins his seven-week unit on the Vietnam War by projecting slides of the Vietnam Veterans Memorial in Washington, D.C., on the wall. His students scan the thousands of names chiseled into the V-shaped memorial's black granite walls and react. His students are moved much as those who visit what has become America's wailing wall.

This incident illustrates the impact that the art that has come out of the war can have on students. In fact, Freedman (1985) argues that the Vietnam War was the first war fought on television and to a rock-and-roll soundtrack. It is because of this that Freedman maintains that it is through art, particularly visual and sound, that we may come to understand the war and its aftermath. In addition, because the war was fought on television and to a rock-and-roll beat, the literature of the war reflects these influences. Therefore, having students do research on the music, dance, art, and photography of the war contributes to their understanding of the literature they study. This activity is designed with these points in mind and is based on suggestions from Matlaw (1988) and DallaGrana (1988).

Begin the activity by passing out the assignment, "Vietnam and the Arts" (see appendix, p. 153). After going over the assignment and topics, give students some time to think about the topics before picking one. While students might do this assignment on their own, I recommend that they do it in pairs or small groups, particularly if the library has limited materials available. It may be useful to assign students to pairs or small groups based on their interest in particular topics. The final reports could be due either while students are studying significant works or as a final activity at the end of a unit or course.

This activity works in a number of ways. First, many of the topics have tremendous appeal to students. For example, students who are interested in rock-and-roll are fascinated to discover how this music reflects the sentiments of the antiwar movement during the 1960s. They are equally fascinated to discover how the music of Bruce Springsteen reflects the changing attitudes of Americans toward those who served in Vietnam. In addition, as they examine the music in light of the literature they are studying, they discover a number of important connections. For example, in reading Tim O'Brien's memoir *If I Die in a Combat Zone*, they note that O'Brien was opposed to the war and yet rejected the call by the antiwar movement to resist the draft or desert the military. They also note that while his memoir is not necessarily an antiwar book, it nevertheless asks readers to consider whether the war was worth the cost. Students are able to connect the literature with art and see how these media in turn reflect the ideological civil war that raged across the land and led to a questioning of the national character. In addition, they see how the art and literature speak to the aftermath of the war and how the war continues to have an impact on their lives.

One variation on the activity is to have students do part of their reports in writing. For example, you might have them answer the questions pertaining to how the art that they researched is reflected in the literature read in class.

Burning Tracers: Teaching Poetry

Some of the best poetry of the Vietnam War seems to function on at least two levels. First, it contains a sense of the need to preserve and capture the experience of Vietnam in all its terrible immediacy. At the same time, it seems to suggest new possibilities of meaning within some larger context of vision common to us all (Beidler 1982). For many elementary and secondary students who often have difficulty interpreting poetry, the very nature of this poetry makes it quite accessible. Students are drawn to the poetry because the experience is so immediate, and as they wrestle with a poem they discover that there is, so to speak, an experience beneath the experience.

The purpose of the following activity is to have students discover some of the themes common in the poetry of the Vietnam War and to interpret the meaning beneath the experience, or, in other words, to make inferences regarding the poets' comments or generalizations about the war. Students also practice examining how Vietnam War writers use language to convey meaning, which should help students when they study longer works.

I would suggest the following procedures for having students work with poetry. Begin with the poem "Fragment: 5 September 1967" (see appendix, p. 155). Read it aloud or ask for a student volunteer to read. Next, have students work on the discussion questions individually for about fifteen minutes (questions are adapted from Carter 1989). Then, using these questions as a guide, lead a class discussion of the poem. The goal of the discussion is for students to generate possible statements of the poet's comment or generalization, refine them so that an effective statement is achieved, and examine how the poet uses language to achieve meaning. After the class discussion has reached closure, hand out the group of poems, "Burning Tracers: Vietnam War Poems" (see appendix, p. 157). In small, heterogeneous groups of three to five, students work together to produce a statement of the poet's generalization about the war in each poem and an explanation of how language is used to achieve meaning. They should discuss the evidence in the poem that leads them to their conclusions. Give each group a dictionary and remind students to find meanings of all words with which they are unfamiliar.

When all groups have finished, lead a class discussion of their analyses. You might have a student from each group put on the blackboard or an overhead transparency the comment his or her group produced for each poem. You might focus on having students identify the best statement for each poem and defend their choices. Most often each group will have produced somewhat different comments. Whether the differences are slight or extreme, lively discussion ensues as students defend their choices and challenge others.

As students defend their choices, they must refer back to the poems to support their interpretations. It is during the course of this activity that students are often struck by how these poets use language to convey meaning. For example, many students are fascinated by the unorthodox comparisons, the stark descriptions of life and death in Vietnam, and the mix of soldiers' slang, militarese, and common, everyday objects to convey meaning.

The small-group and whole-class discussions help students come to a more sophisticated understanding of the poets' comments about the war and of how they use language to convey meaning. Starting with a whole class discussion of a single poem is also important. The teacher provides structure and support when students are unfamiliar with this poetry and the thinking involved. In a sense, the teacher, along with the class, models the process of interpreting a poem. Then, once students have had a little practice, they are prepared to try interpreting a few in a more independent situation.

I often have students study poetry and other short works prior to reading a novel or other longer work because it allows them to deal with important themes and concepts in small amounts prior to having to deal with them in a complex work. In a sense, the shorter works serve as a means to introduce themes and concepts and give them practice in interpreting them. This introduction and practice thus makes it easier for students to interpret themes in complex works. In fact, Smith and Hillocks (1988) cite literary theory and research which suggests that careful grouping and sequencing of texts in the manner described here can provide students with the kind of knowledge that will enable them to interpret increasingly complex texts. The poems in the activities that follow have been selected with this instructional purpose in mind. They reflect a range of themes and concepts which students will likely encounter in longer works.

A possible follow-up writing assignment is to have students write a short composition explaining the poet's comment or generalization about the Vietnam War in a poem that has not been discussed in class. Hand out the composition assignment for the poem "Coming Home" (see appendix, p. 160). Students write a composition in which they (1) explain the comment or generalization the poet makes about the war and (2) argue, through effective use of evidence from the poem, their reasons for interpreting the meaning this way.

When they bring in their rough drafts, divide students into small groups to evaluate each other's papers. In response groups, each student reads his or her paper aloud, and then the group members work together to go over the draft and improve it. The group should discuss each paper with the writer and explain reasons for the comments made. After the group discussions, the writers should have an opportunity to make revisions and a final copy to turn in to the teacher.

On Patrol: Activities for Short Stories

Eleven or twelve years ago, when I first started teaching the literature of the Vietnam War with high school students, I had difficulty coming up with even two good short stories from readily available sources. Now, there are so many excellent and available short stories, that I have difficulty deciding which ones to use. As with other modern short stories, those that focus on the Vietnam War use a variety of techniques and deal with a wide range of themes and issues. At the heart of many of the best is the unique way that the language and narrative style convey the confusion and absurdity of war.

As with poetry, I often have students study a number of short stories before they read a major work. In this way I can give them experience and practice in analyzing the themes and concepts they will encounter in major works, and I use the opportunity to study short stories as a chance to examine how Vietnam War writers use language to convey meaning.

The activities that follow illustrate different ways that you might set up instruction to achieve different instructional purposes. However, before using these stories or any literature dealing with the Vietnam War, it is important for the teacher to examine the selections carefully and decide whether they are appropriate for a given situation. Some selections might be too graphic for certain students and communities. Some writers use obscene language to convey their experience of the war's brutality, injustice, suffering, and death. Others simply reproduce the language of the moment to re-create the situation accurately. In either case, the teacher should be aware of potential problems with some selections and preview materials before using them in the classroom.

On Patrol #1: Choices

Irony is a key element of fiction, and it is a technique used in some of the best Vietnam War short stories. Writers use irony to show the madness, confusion, brutality, courage, fear, dying, and brotherhood of war. I have used this activity which is adapted from Johannessen (1990) a number of times to help students understand how irony works and what these writers tell us about war through their use of irony.

I use two stories that challenge the media-molded myths and images that many students have about the war: Tim O'Brien's "Centurion," from his memoir *If I Die in a Combat Zone*, which has been published separately as a short story, and Robin Moore's "We Have Met the Enemy," from *Combat Pay*, his collection of short stories. Both stories suggest the madness of a war in which decent men must confront the inescapable brutality of war. In O'Brien's story, students discover that brutality is the inescapable outcome when a raid on a village turns up an enemy weapon but no visible enemy. In Moore's story, they see how acts of self-preservation can result in brutality. Both stories make clear that the realities of the Vietnam War are far different from Hollywood's romanticized and glorified versions. They suggest to students the dangers of believing in these images and myths.

I usually begin with the "Vietnam War Opinionnaire" (pp. 145–46). Once we have discussed most or all of the statements on the opinionnaire, I have students read the two stories. Then I divide the class into small, mixed groups and ask them to determine from evidence in the stories how the narrator and Bates would have reacted had they been in the situation Hucks and Leland were confronted with in "We Have Met the Enemy" and how Hucks and Leland would have reacted had they been in the situation the narrator and Bates faced in "Centurion."

In O'Brien's story, the narrator and Bates are faced with a difficult situation. The officers in the unit randomly pull three old men out of a hut, tie them up, gag them, and bind them to saplings in the center of the unit's perimeter, using the logic that the enemy guerrillas will not attack that night because their fathers have been taken prisoner. The narrator feels compassion for the old men. He thinks they may be innocent and knows that in the morning they will be tortured for information about the enemy. Yet he does almost nothing to help them. He seems to be unable to do anything significant about the brutality of the incident, accepting it as the price of survival in a crazy war.

Hucks and Leland, the characters in Moore's story, are in a very different situation. Cut off from their unit during a fire fight and being pursued by the enemy, they move to a position along a cliff. Suddenly, they see a shadowy figure run into a cave near their position. Believing the figure to be an enemy soldier, they throw a grenade into the cave. When they go inside to investigate, they discover the body of a young Vietnamese girl about ten years old.

Once students have come up with their conclusions, evidence, and explanations, I have the class reassemble to discuss their findings. As the groups begin reporting their ideas, students are surprised to discover that it would not have made any difference. Most agree that Moore's characters, like O'Brien's, would have done little to help the old men, and that O'Brien's characters probably would have killed the shadowy figure that ran into the cave. Once students understand that these different characters probably would have reacted the same in either situation, they are prepared to deal with irony.

I ask students to return to their small groups. They attempt to explain why these characters would have reacted the same way in either situation and why the outcome in each incident is brutality. They also respond to the question, "What are O'Brien and Moore telling us about the Vietnam War?"

After working out responses to these questions in small groups, the class reassembles to discuss and debate its findings. As we discuss the stories, students begin to formulate important conclusions. They realize, for example, that O'Brien is not criticizing the narrator of his story for doing very little to help the old men who are tortured. They see the irony of the situation—had the patrol not taken the three old men prisoner, they probably would have been attacked by the enemy. Students recognize the lack of choices in such a situation; the patrol takes the old men prisoner and tortures them because, as Bates tells the narrator, "This is war, my friend. You don't find a weapon and just walk away." Students perceive that, even for those with a strong sense of right and wrong, cruelty and brutality are inevitable outcomes of war.

Having students study stories like these helps them see the realities of the Vietnam War. It is very difficult for most students to continue to hang on to their oversimplified good-guys-against-the-bad-guys image of the war. In addition, studying stories like these helps prepare students for more complex works dealing with the war. For example, students realize that the only victory in these stories is survival. They echo the hollow conclusion Philip Caputo makes in *A Rumor of War* when he leaves Vietnam: "We had done nothing more than endure. We had survived, and that was our only victory."

If you have used the opinionnaire with these stories, have students refer back to it and compare their responses with their observations about the stories. Often opinions have changed. One student made this comment: "In this one Vietnam War movie, they made the war look like it would be sort of fun and exciting, but in these stories it's just awful, really awful!"

As a follow-up, I ask students to read on their own another story that involves the Vietnam War and that uses irony to convey its meaning. Then I ask them to write an interpretation of the story. I use either Wayne Karlin's "Extract," from *Free Fire Zone: Short Stories by Vietnam Veterans* or Robert L. Perea's "Small Arms Fire," from *Cuentos Chicanos: A Short Story Anthology* (see the list of selected and annotated resources, pp. 101–38). This follow-up reinforces skills students have developed in reading and analyzing "Centurion" and "We Have Met the Enemy." Another possible follow-up writing activity is to have students select one or two of the items from the opinionnaire and discuss how their image or perceptions of the war have changed as a result of reading the stories. This follow-up serves as a means of reinforcing the impact that the literature has had on them and to explore further their responses.

On Patrol #2: "Night March" by Tim O'Brien

A number of excellent short stories offer opportunities to examine character development and see the thoughts, feelings, and experiences of those involved in the war. One such story that works well with most secondary and undergraduate students is Tim O'Brien's "Night March," from his novel, *Going after Cacciato*, which has also been published separately as a short story.

The story focuses on the theme of fear and imagination. The imagination is shown to be an important faculty in both mental and physical survival in war. The author also explores what fear feels like and what it does to Paul Berlin, an average infantry soldier.

The story takes place on young Paul Berlin's first night in Vietnam. His platoon is on a night march. The narrator takes readers into Paul Berlin's mind as the platoon moves through the hedgerows and rice paddies. O'Brien shows readers how fear and imagination work on Paul, and how, by the end of the story, Paul comes to see that the fear never goes away but that he would be better at handling it tomorrow.

This story speaks directly to some of the misconceptions students often have about war. Many students do not understand that, for the common infantry soldier, most wars primarily consist of long periods of boredom interrupted suddenly by brutal moments of intense action. It is during those long stretches of boredom that a soldier's imagination and fear can take over with possible negative results. This story helps students see that war is not continual nonstop action and adventure.

The story also deals with an important characteristic of the literature of the Vietnam War that distinguishes it from the literature of other wars. In World Wars I and II, the average age of men who served was twenty-six. In Vietnam, the average was much younger: a mere nineteen years old. This means that the soldiers must be portrayed differently from those in other wars. O'Brien is careful to make this difference clear in his story.

I have students read the story on their own (again, most often after having done one or more of the introductory activities described earlier). Then I have students answer the "'Night March' Discussion Questions" (see appendix, p. 161) either on their own or in small groups. After students have finished working on their answers, I lead a class discussion using the questions as a guide in helping students understand what O'Brien is saying about imagination and fear. For example, students come to understand that fear is a constant companion of the soldier and that the key question is not that a soldier not be afraid, but rather that he learn to control his feelings of fear. They also realize that imagination has a double edge to it: it can help a soldier control fear, or it can run wild and cause a soldier to lose control.

As a follow-up, I have students write an imaginative piece describing Paul Berlin's second day in Vietnam. In it, they must answer the following questions: Does Paul do a better job of controlling his fear? If so, how? What things does Paul imagine during his second day? Does his imagination help him control his fear or cause him to lose control of it? Other possible follow-up assignments include having students write about their own fears and how they try to deal with them, or having them write a paper in which they must explain why they either agree or disagree with O'Brien that there are different kinds of fears.

On Patrol #3: Vietnam Lexicon

Gilman argues that what makes the literature of the Vietnam War unique from the literature of other wars is what he calls "the paradoxical paradigm of nomenclature" (1988, 62). He claims that the genre of science fiction falls closest to Vietnam fiction on the matter of language. Yet he indicates that it is the language that gives Vietnam War fiction its remarkable intensity and makes it so appealing. Arguing in a similar vein, Anisfield describes the language in some Vietnam War fiction as "intensified beyond the colloquialisms found in standard narratives" (1988, 58). She explains that the Vietnam War had its own lexicon which is part of the literature. The lexicon consists of a combination of Americanized foreign words and phrases, military jargon, rock music lyrics, and a unique in-country vocabulary derived from various other sources. Anisfield argues that writers use this Vietnam lexicon to create a fictional environment which shows the physical and psychic atmosphere of the war and to give them more avenues through which to comment on the war.

While the Vietnam lexicon may be what makes the literature unique, it can also be a major stumbling block for many students. However, with a little practice, most students can become quite adept at figuring out this sometimes confusing vocabulary. With a little practice, terms like a "two-digit midget" (a soldier with 99 days or less left on his or her tour of duty in Vietnam), "LZ" (a landing zone for helicopters), or "zapped" (to get killed) become as familiar to them as a word like "nerd." Once students have some understanding of the linquistic environment of Vietnam, they are much better able to understand what writers are saying about the war.

Having students work with the language in short stories before they read a major work makes good instructional sense. On more than one occasion in the past, I have made the mistake of thinking that the glossary provided by some Vietnam War writers would be all students would need to comprehend the language. Now, I have the class work with a short story or two that rely on the Vietnam lexicon before we tackle a longer work.

I begin by handing out the "Vietnam Lexicon" sheet (see appendix, p. 163) and going over the explanation and examples of each type of jargon. Then I tell students that we are going to make our own glossary of Vietnam lexicon. I hand out a story that relies on this language to convey meaning. A good one to use is Larry Heinemann's "The First Clean Fact" (see the annotated list of selected resources). Many other stories and anthologized excerpts will work just as well. Three other stories that work well for this activity are Ronald J. Glasser's "Mayfield," from *365 Days*, Tom Suddick's "Caduceus," from *A Few Good Men*, and Tom Mayer's "A Birth in the Delta," from *The Weary Falcon* (all three of these selections are also in *Touring Nam: The Vietnam War Reader* [see the annotated list of resources for more information]). Also, nearly any anthologized selection from Michael Herr's *Dispatches* will work well.

Once I have handed out the story, we begin reading the story aloud. After a few paragraphs, we begin to run into jargon: terms such as "busting jungle," "pungi pits," "Fire Base," "zonked out," and "zip." As we encounter each term, I ask if anyone in the class knows or thinks he or she may know what the word means. Usually, we get about one-fourth of our words defined in this fashion. If no one in the class knows, we go back to the text and see if we can figure it out by looking at context clues in the passage. As we arrive at definitions, I have students write the word and its definition in their lists. About halfway through the story, I tell them to finish it on their own and to list words and definitions as they read. I also have them make a separate list for any words they are unable to define.

Once students have finished the story and their lists, I lead a class discussion of the story beginning with their lists of words. In going over their definitions, we encounter key words like "Crispy Critters" and "incoming round" which lead directly to the heart of the story—"the first clean fact" is that an entire unit was wiped out in a single artillery blast and all died screaming with no idea of why they were in the place they died. As we discuss the author's use of the Vietnam lexicon in the story, students begin to see how he uses this language to show the full horror of death in Vietnam. Once we have finished, I tell students to keep their glossary in their notebooks for future reference.

As a follow-up, you might have students read another story on their own that uses the Vietnam lexicon to convey meaning and have them explain how the use of this language contributes to the meaning of the story. This follow-up serves as a means to check students' understanding of the analytical skills they have learned.

In doing this activity with this story or others, it is important to keep in mind that the language used is often graphic and obscene. However, strong language is as much a part of the Vietnam lexicon as Americanized foreign words. This language is in part what gives the literature its own sound and tone: it helped those who served in the war to distance themselves from the horror and to describe and share their experiences, and it helps readers of this literature to hear and feel what it was like to be in Vietnam. Therefore, common Vietnam lingo such as "REMF" (rear echelon motherfucker) or "FNG" (fucking new guy) will appear in some of these works. The teacher needs to decide what is appropriate for a given situation. Without losing the actual meaning, many acronyms might be handled as follows: "REMF": a base camp support troop; "FNG": a new man in country.

However, it is equally important to remember that to understand the war students need to examine the linguistic currency in which the war was fought. Christie notes that "as for language, perhaps students need to see more graphic language and imagery in contexts where they occur with good reason: perhaps we all need to study that language and those images for what they say to us about our world and the uses of language, anyway" (1989, 37).

On Patrol #4: With the Enemy

In the theory and research section, I described how one of my students confused Korea with Vietnam. This incident pointed out to me that one of the more confusing aspects of the war for students is exactly who was fighting whom. Despite the simplistic good-guys-against-the-bad-guys view that comes across in Hollywood's version of the war, knowing who was enemy and who was "friendly" was often very confusing for those who fought it. For many years and in many places in Vietnam, the war was primarily a guerrilla war. A simple peasant farmer by day might be a Vietcong by night. An innocent-looking peasant village might be the headquarters for an enemy unit.

Unfortunately, there has not been much fiction written about the enemy. However, there are two very fine and readily available short stories that provide a fascinating look at the enemy and reveal cultural differences that some scholars say is at least partially responsible for our inability to win the war. These are David

Huddle's "The Interrogation of the Prisoner Bung by Mister Hawkins and Sergeant Tree," and Larry Rottmann's "Thi Bong Dzu," both originally published in *Free Fire Zone: Short Stories by Vietnam Veterans* and also in *Vietnam Anthology: American War Literature* (see annotated list of resources).

Huddle's story focuses on an interrogation of a Vietcong suspect, Bung, by an American advisor, Mister Hawkins, and his Vietnamese interpreter, Sergeant Tree. As the story develops, it becomes clear that Mister Hawkins has little understanding of the Vietnamese he is dealing with and that Sergeant Tree is as corrupt and incompetent as the government he works for. The prisoner appears to be nothing more than an ignorant peasant farmer. Once Bung is released, however, the reader learns that he is in fact a Vietcong soldier. He has memorized the camp where he was being held and is now planning an attack on it.

Rottmann's story focuses on a day in the life of a young Vietcong soldier. The soldier, who is eleven years old, spends his day working in the rice paddies with other villagers. The reader sees what his family life is like, sees him harvesting rice, and sees his reaction to Americans and their equipment that pass by him during the day. The reader learns that the boy is excited about his birthday party planned for the following day. That night the boy prepares to join his unit for action against the Americans. Shortly after the boy leaves home, he makes a fatal mistake: instead of concentrating on being alert for the enemy, he begins thinking about his birthday party. He fails to note the warning signs that the Americans have set up an ambush, and as a result, he walks right into the ambush and is killed.

Begin by having students read both stories. Then pass out the "'With the Enemy' Discussion Questions" (see appendix, p. 166). You might have students work on the questions individually or in small groups. Once they have finished the questions, lead a class discussion of their answers. Both stories usually have a powerful effect on students. They are often surprised to discover how clever Bung was at playing the role of the ignorant peasant farmer and how easily the American and Vietnamese officials were taken in by him. They are equally surprised that Dzu was only eleven years old. As students discuss the stories, they begin to understand who the Vietnamese people are and how the cultural and psychological differences between the Americans and Vietnamese produced significant gaps in understanding. They begin to see how these gaps may have contributed to our inability to win the war.

As a follow-up, the teacher might have students write a composition explaining which of the two stories had the greater impact on them and why. Another possibility is to have students read on their own another story dealing with the enemy and then have them write an interpretation of the story. You might have them read Nguyen Sang's "The Ivory Comb," from *The Ivory Comb,* and in *Fragment from a Lost Diary and Other Stories: Women of Asia, Africa, and Latin America,* or Asa Baber's "Ambush," which is in *Touring Nam, Vietnam Anthology: American War Literature, and Writing under Fire: Stories of the Vietnam War* (see annotated list of resources). This last follow-up reinforces what students have learned in reading and analyzing "Thi Bong Dzu" and "The Interrogation of the Prisoner Bung by Mister Hawkins and Sergeant Tree."

On Patrol #5: The War at Home

As the war in Vietnam escalated, so did the fragmentations and polarization of people at home. Fortunately, there are some fine short stories that examine the effects of the war on the homefront. However, the problem for many students is that their knowledge of events that took place at home during the Vietnam era is as poor, if not poorer, than their knowledge of the war in Vietnam. In fact, the mythologized Hollywood version of the war that many students have acquired from popular films and elsewhere seems to have left them with nothing more than a rather vague disdain for those who were involved in the antiwar movement. Clearly, students need to examine the impact of the war at home and legacies of the war.

I use five stories that examine the war at home and some of the costs and consequences of the war: Breece D'J Pancake's "The Honored Dead," Karen Jay Fowler's "Letters from Home," Judith Rascoe's "Soldier, Soldier," Kim Stanley Robinson's "The Monument," and Michael Rossman's "The Day We Named Our Child We Had Fish for Dinner." (See annotated list of resources for sources for these and other possible stories to use in this activity.)

One way to begin is with the "Vietnam War Opinionnaire" (pp. 145–46). Follow the procedures described for using the opinionnaire. Another way to introduce some of the ideas and concepts students will encounter in these stories is to play some protest songs from the '60s and '70s and discuss their responses to this music and the themes. Some possibilities are: Stephen Stills's "For What It's Worth," Buffy St. Marie's "Universal Soldier," Neil Young's "Ohio," Joe McDonald's "I-Feel-Like-I'm-Fixin'-to-Die-Rag," and Arlo Guthrie's "Alice's Restaurant."

Then tell students that they are going to be reading some stories that deal with the war at home. A good story to start with is David Rossman's "The Day We Named Our Child We Had Fish for Dinner." The story focuses on a Berkeley, California, couple who are actively involved in the antiwar movement and what happens to the two during the first few days in May 1970 after the invasion of Cambodia. The narrator reflects on his involvement in the movement, the events that are taking place across the nation, and the tragedy at Kent State. He realizes for the first time that he might not survive the present situation, and he notes the growing fragmentation of himself and the country. He decides in the end that if the country survives, everyone will be better as a result.

After students have finished reading the story, lead a class discussion focusing on the narrator, the events the narrator describes, and the effects of the events on the characters in the story and on the country. The discussion should lead students to understand why the narrator believes he must protest against the war and the effects of the war on individuals and society. It might also be worthwhile to have students discuss to what extent the effects discussed in the story are still with us today.

The next step is to assign students to small groups and have each group read one or two of the other short stories just listed. Try to set up the readings so that each story is being read by at least two groups. As an alternative to the traditional study guide, have students fill out the "The War at Home: Short Story Chart" (see appendix, p. 167). Using Rossman's story as a model, go over how to fill in the chart, encouraging students to add additional details from Rossman's story to the chart. (The information in the chart is from the excerpted version of the story in *Vietnam Voices*.) Then have students read their assigned story or stories, and meet in their small groups to discuss and add to their charts. Once the small groups have finished their charts, have them report their findings to the rest of the class. The rest of the students should complete their charts from the small-group reports.

Ideally, more than one group will have read each story. As a result, discussion is encouraged as groups challenge or question information and ideas reported by other groups. With their charts filled in, students are ready for the next step. Lead a class discussion focusing on the effects of the war at home as expressed by these authors. Which individuals seem to have suffered the most? Why? Are there segments of society that seem to have suffered the effects more than others? How? Why? Which of these effects are still with us today? Why? How might we deal with them? Many students are surprised by some of the long-term effects of the war. For example, they see that the narrator in Pancake's story is still troubled by the fact, many years after the war, that he used a trick to avoid the draft. In addition, they see that the narrator and his father had a serious disagreement about the war and that differences in views on the war led to a break in his relationship with his father. In addition, students come to realize that just because people did not fight in the war does not mean that they were not affected by it. Students see that those who protested against the war or who avoided or evaded the draft are in many ways just as haunted by the war as those who served in Vietnam. This discussion is usually at a high level because of students' previous work in completing the charts. They have considerable information to draw from in discussing the effects of the war at home.

As a follow-up, the teacher might have students write a composition explaining which of the effects from the war in the story or stories they read (or any from the chart) are still with us today, and how they think the nation might overcome or resolve these legacies that have had such an impact on individuals and society. Another possible follow-up assignment is to have students discuss orally or in writing whether they believe, as a number of politicians and generals have stated, that the war in the Persian Gulf has laid to rest the ghosts of Vietnam. They should also explain why they believe as they do about this issue. Finally, now that students know a bit more about some of the effects of the war on the home front, they might write about the impact of the war on them personally, their families, and their communities. These assignments ask students to do some additional thinking about the effects of the war at home. In addition, this activity and the follow-up assignments should help students realize that even though the Vietnam War was fought thousands of miles away from the shores of America, it had a traumatic impact on the entire country.

Acts of War: Drama and Film

A number of excellent dramas have been written dealing with the Vietnam War. Unfortunately, they are often difficult to obtain, and very few of them have been anthologized. In addition, many of these plays pose other teaching problems. For example, David Rabe's *Sticks and Bones* is certainly one of the best plays to come out of the war.

However, Rabe's writing is intentionally crazy, shocking, and symbolic. The same is true of Tom Cole's excellent one-act play, *Medal of Honor Rag*. In short, besides being difficult to obtain, these plays are too difficult for most students to understand. Therefore, I suggest teaching plays such as the one I use in "Acts of War #1: Drama," which are readily available and more accessible to the majority of students.

Unlike the situation with dramas, there are so many outstanding, award-winning documentary and feature-length films available that there simply is no reason why they should not be a part of any unit or course dealing with the Vietnam War. In addition, as Christie argues,

> Films are especially useful for a unit (or course) on myth: from John Wayne in *The Green Berets* (1968) to Robert Duvall as Colonel Kilgore in *Apocalypse Now* (1979), America has consistently projected potent mythic images from Vietnam onto the movie screen. . . . More recent offerings like *Rambo* and even *Platoon* further that mythic legacy as they indicate how thoroughly the war (like all wars?) became itself the material of new cultural myth. (1989, 36)

Finally, one of the inevitable problems teachers encounter in trying to teach a unit or course on the Vietnam War is that because the war was so long and there are so many issues involved in the war, no one work or even a good collection of works could possibly do justice to most or all of the issues. However, using documentary and feature-length films enables the teacher to do a good job of covering most or all of the major topics and issues related to the war.

Acts of War #1: Drama

A few years ago I was browsing in a used bookstore when I ran across a copy of *Great Television Plays,* edited by William I. Kaufman (New York: Dell, 1969). In it is a play about the Vietnam War produced by "CBS Playhouse Presents: 'The Final War of Ollie Winter'" by Ronald Ribman. When I tried the play with my high school students, I was pleased to discover that they really enjoyed it. Since then I have talked to a number of teachers who use this play in their teaching. Recently, in fact, one seventh-grade teacher told me that he has been using it for many years with his students.

The play is interesting for several reasons. First, it takes place early in the war, 1963, before America had committed large-scale ground forces to the war. This gives students an opportunity to see what it was like for those soldiers who were in Vietnam during this stage of the war. The hero, Master Sergeant Ollie Winter, is an advisor to the South Vietnamese Army. He is an experienced soldier who fought in World War II and Korea. In addition, he is black, and throughout the play he tries to remain human—and humane— within the horror of the Vietnam War. As the play progresses, the audience comes to realize that despite the injustice he has experienced in his own country, he remains loyal to the United States. Finally, as he moves through the events that will ultimately result in his own death, Ollie increasingly reaches out for the underlying goodness of life. He comes to value the life of his enemy more than is militarily prudent; he hopes that out of all the present suffering may come love and a new life.

Ollie is also the only American in the play, as Ribman takes the audience into the Vietnamese culture. We see an inept South Vietnamese Army lieutenant who ignores Ollie's sound military advice and, as a result, dies along with the rest of his platoon in a Vietcong ambush. We meet a village chief who is caught between the corrupt South Vietnamese government and the brutal Vietcong. We meet a Vietcong soldier and a young South Vietnamese woman who are so caught up in their own political rhetoric that all they see is hatred for one another. Students are given an interesting look at the political and cultural environment of Vietnam from the Vietnamese point of view.

I find that the play is best read aloud. I assign students to read the parts of various characters. There are seventeen parts, and with someone reading the stage directions, most of the students in a class will have a part. It takes two to three days in class. I usually stop the class after Act II and discuss what we have read to that point. On the second day we read Acts III and IV and then discuss the rest of the play. In the discussions, I focus on the Vietnamese people and why many Americans came to see the Vietnamese as less than human. We also examine the role of blacks and other minorities who served in Vietnam. I ask students why it might have been more difficult for minorities to fight in the war. Finally, we discuss how Ollie changed during the play and what caused those changes.

As a follow-up, students might do some research on minorities and women who served in Vietnam. They might make brief oral reports to the class on their findings and/or write short reports of what they learn. Also, now that they know something about the Vietnamese people, they might also do research on the Vietnamese and other Southeast Asian peoples who came to the United States after the war.

Acts of War #2: A Documentary Film: Letters from the Combat Zone

In all the years I have taught the literature of the Vietnam War to my high school and college students, nothing has had quite the impact as the excellent documentary film *Dear America: Letters Home from Vietnam* (see annotated list of resources). In fact, in my discussions with other teachers who have used this and other films in their units and courses, there is general agreement that this film is one of the anchors. They might change many other things in their units and courses, but this film is one of the mainstays.

Directed by Bill Couturie and produced by the Couturie Company and Vietnam Veterans Ensemble Theater Company, the film stands out as perhaps the best documentary on the Vietnam War. It is based on a book of veterans' letters home and was originally an HBO cable-TV special that won so much praise it was released and shown in theaters around the country.

The film is so powerful that teaching it demands special handling. The first time I used the film I tried to have a discussion as soon as the film was over. I quickly discovered that my students were so moved that they were unable to speak. One young lady tried and immediately burst into tears and ran out of the classroom. Now, I move slowly and carefully.

Another problem I have had with the film is that it is so powerful that it is sometimes difficult to get students to think critically. This activity attempts to help students be thoughtful about what they view.

Ideally, the film should be shown from beginning to end without interruption. Unfortunately, it is too long to be viewed in a single class period. At 84 minutes, it is difficult to squeeze it into two class periods if there is anything else going on. However, if the teacher is unable to show it in its entirety, I recommend squeezing it into two days. Give a very brief introduction on the first day and move into the film. Stop near the end of the period and answer any questions students might have. On the second day, I suggest backing the film up a bit so that it runs to nearly the end of the period. Then show the rest of the film to the end. I suggest running the credits at the end instead of cutting it off to have a discussion. Tell students that the class will discuss the film the following day. Let students come down from the emotional impact of the film. My experience has been that students will sit quietly when the film is over.

On the following day I hand out the activity sheet "Some Themes from *Dear America: Letters Home from Vietnam*" (see appendix, p. 168). Although this activity can be done individually by students, it usually works best in small, heterogeneous groups of three to five students so that group members can help each other remember important statements from letters read in the film. The sheet is designed to help students identify themes and quotations from letters that support the themes. I usually do the first one with the class so that everyone understands what to do. I explain that for theme 4 they are to decide what theme the quotations suggest and think of two quotations that would go along with the two I have provided. For theme 5 they are to think of another theme or issue from the film that they think is important and also think of at least two quotations that support it.

After students have completed this assignment, I assemble the class to discuss findings. As the groups report and we discuss their answers, students begin to understand some of the themes and issues presented in the film. The most interesting part of the discussion comes with themes 4 and 5. Although other themes and issues are possible for theme 4, students often come up with something like "the daily life of the soldier was boring, physically and emotionally exhausting and dangerous with moments of absolute terror." For the theme and evidence they must do on their own (theme 5), students generate evidence for themes such as "soldiers killed to survive and found some meaning in the experience"; "winning medals for heroism became meaningless"; "those at home seemed not to understand what the war was like"; and "politicians and generals use the language of winning, while we are actually losing the war."

Once we have discussed the themes and issues brought out in the film, I turn the discussion to the images presented in the film. I ask students for their personal responses: What affected you the most? How did you feel? As we discuss their responses, I am always struck by the depth of responses. Some students are moved by how young and innocent the soldiers all looked when they first arrived and how they changed into hardened killers. Others are angry at how blind people were back in the United States to the reality of the war. Others are struck by the insanity of the war. Most of them can recall and describe specific images from the film to support their responses.

As a follow-up writing activity or as an alternative to the discussion of students' personal responses, I use the writing assignment, "Responding to *Dear America: Letters Home from Vietnam*" (see appendix, p. 170). The assignment directs students to write on one of the topics and to use images, words, and/or ideas from the film to answer the questions for each topic. In other words, it reinforces the analytical skills introduced in this activity but also encourages them to explore their personal responses to the film.

The following excerpts from student papers illustrate the powerful impact the film had on them and how their previous work helped them generate responses that they could support with evidence from the film:

> Just seeing the pictures of the scared faces as they awaited the enemy made me think about Vietnam and also gave me a deeper understanding of how boys were forced to become men (many of them before their time). The one nurse said it best in her letter home when she said, "They're just kids, 18, 19 . . . ." These young men lost their innocence fighting for the good of the U.S.A., and I think that this was very courageous and noble.

> Something that struck me was who the soldiers saw as the enemy. The answer was practically everyone and everything. These men "had to kill to survive." The enemy already had the advantage of fighting on their turf and the one thing we could not give them was opportunity. Before I really learned about the Vietnam War I used to wonder how our men could be so cruel as to kill children and families. The fact that the enemy used them to get to us made my skin crawl. No wonder "it's so very easy to kill in a war."

> One letter which touched me the most was when the soldier wrote of how you can have no friends in Vietnam because when you become close to a person they get killed and this hurts you even more.

The following student was so moved by the film that she began asking herself the most important question of all:

> After viewing the film, the questions that went through my head were "Why do we go to war and is it worth it?" One soldier was asked, "Do you think that it is worth it?" And his reply was, "They say we are fighting for something but I don't know." After seeing how the soldiers suffered from day-to-day, wondering when they will go home or even if they will still be alive the next day, doesn't put a doubt in my mind and I don't think that it is worth it.

Clearly, the film has a powerful impact, and the activity helps students generate thoughtful responses to the film. It is also worthwhile to have students share their responses with their peers. They might read their papers in small groups and/or to the whole class. Small groups might be directed to identify the image or images that had the greatest impact. Then each group might share those images with the class. Discussion might focus on why these images had such an impact.

Acts of War #3: A Documentary Film: Frontline America

If students are to understand the Vietnam War, it is important for them to examine the war at home. The antiwar movement is as much a part of the Vietnam War as the experiences of those who fought in the jungles and mountains of Southeast Asia. In fact, as the war dragged on and escalated, the antiwar movement grew from a few radical students and intellectuals to a mass movement with supporters from all walks of life, including Vietnam veterans. What many students fail to appreciate is that the polarization of political views over the war nearly tore the country apart.

To help students understand the antiwar movement and some of the effects of the war on the nation, I often use one of the many excellent documentary films that are available. One possibility is to use one or more of the one-hour segments from the PBS series, *Vietnam: A Television History*. For example, segment #11, "Homefront USA," focuses on the war at home and explores the impact of the war on the nation. Another possibility is to have students view one or more of the forty-nine-minute segments from the documentary series, *Vietnam: The Ten Thousand Day War*. For example, segment #8, "Frontline America," examines the war on the home front. Either of these possibilities will provide excellent background on the war at home as well as opportunities for examining many of the issues.

However, the best film available for studying the war at home is *Vietnam: The War at Home*. Nominated for the Best Documentary Oscar in 1978, this one-hour-and-forty-minute film presents a wide array of news and interview footage that examines the effects of the Vietnam political ambiguities on the home front. This powerful film concentrates on student activists at the University of Wisconsin and manages, perhaps because of this focus, to have a strong impact on students.

Before showing the film, you might begin by having students discuss what they know about the antiwar/peace movement. Don't be surprised by their lack of knowledge. My experience has been that most students know very little about the subject.

Another possibility is to begin by giving students a number of antiwar slogans from the Vietnam era. You might simply write some or all of the following on the board:

"Make love, not war."

"Give peace a chance."

"Hell no, we won't go."

"War is not healthy for children and other living things."

"What if they gave a war and nobody came?"

"Hey, hey, LBJ, how many kids did you kill today?"

"Ho, Ho, Ho Chi Minh. The N.L.F. is gonna win."

Then ask students if they have ever heard any of the slogans and to explain what they know about them. In addition, ask them to speculate on why those opposed to the war might have used these slogans and phrases, and how they think others might have reacted to them.

Once the class has discussed most or all of the slogans, introduce the film, pointing out that it deals with the antiwar movement and the effects of the war at home. After viewing the film, you might lead a brief class discussion to clarify anything students may not understand in the film.

However, before having a serious discussion of the film, I usually give students the writing assignment, "Thinking about *Vietnam: The War at Home"* (see appendix, p. 171). Based in part on ideas suggested by John Reiff of the University of Michigan and Kirschner and Weisberg (1988), this assignment encourages students to explore their personal reactions to the film. After students have written on one of the topics, I ask them to share their written responses. Then, I lead a class discussion that focuses on their reactions to the film. An interesting variation is to have students meet in small groups to share and discuss their responses. Some students cannot understand why anyone would protest the war. Others, particularly young men who are aware of their obligation to register for the draft, are troubled by the prospect of having to serve in combat in some remote corner of the world. Others wonder for the first time if perhaps the war was wrong and if the cost was too high. Most of them can recall at least one image or statement from the film that left an impression on them.

As a follow-up writing activity, I often have students write a more formal essay based on their response writing and the class discussion. I ask them to use images and statements from the film as support for their viewpoints. Another possible follow-up assignment, suggested by DallaGrana (1988) and Matlaw (1988)— especially if students seem interested in the antiwar movement— is to have them do a little bit of outside research. Have students find the lyrics or a recording of an antiwar song from that era or a more recent song dealing with the war. To help them get started, you might suggest the following possibilities: Pete Seeger's "Last Train to Nuremberg," "Where Have All the Flowers Gone?" "Uncle Ho," and "Masters of War"; Country Joe and the Fish's "I Feel Like I'm Fixin' to Die Rag"; Arlo Guthrie's "Alice's Restaurant"; Phil Ochs and Bob Gibson's "I Ain't Marchin' Any More"; and newer songs like Bob Dylan's "Clean-Cut Kid"; Bruce Springsteen's "Born in the U.S.A."; Dan Daley's "Still in Saigon"; Huey Lewis's "Walking on a Thin Line"; and Billy Joel's "Goodnight Saigon." Have students play the recording or present the lyrics to the class and discuss how the song reflects what they saw in the film or what was happening in the United States at the time the song was popular. Matlaw (1988), who ends her high school history course with a similar assignment, points out that this assignment gives students a new appreciation for music as an indicator of the spirit of the times and its role in social movements.

Acts of War #4: A Feature-Length Film

There is no shortage of readily available, outstanding feature-length films about the Vietnam War (see annotated list of resources). Each time I have taught the literature of the war I have used a different feature-length film. The units and courses outlined in the theory section all include major films. The available motion pictures deal with a surprising variety of themes and topics, from the insanity of the war as portrayed in *Apocalypse Now* to the realistic horror of combat in the jungle in *Platoon*, and from the destruction of our cultural myths in *Born on the Fourth of July* to the destruction of a family in *Coming Home*.

I would argue that there are important reasons for selecting some films over others for inclusion in a unit or course on the Vietnam War. While some might reasonably decide to show *Apocalypse Now* because of its close connection to Joseph Conrad's *Heart of Darkness* and the clear relationship that can be made to past literature, I believe that films like *Platoon, Born on the Fourth of July,* and *Full*

Metal Jacket may have much more to offer students. One of the strengths of these films is that they function within the same linguistic currency that characterizes many of the best works of literature. Students are thus given an opportunity to hear the language and to examine the very nature and power of language. For example, in these films, students vividly see how the language of the war, the Vietnam vernacular, helped the war's participants distance themselves emotionally from what they were experiencing.

More important, teaching one of these films provides a unique opportunity to explore a major issue that connects the Vietnam generation to the children of the Vietnam generation. Bryan (1984) notes that the soldiers who fought in Vietnam were different from the soldiers who served in previous wars. He argues that myths and media images had formed the latter's views about war. Doherty (1988) agrees with Bryan and says, "A true son of Hollywood and television, the Vietnam soldier was weaned on mass-mediated fantasies of World War II combat" (25). He takes his argument a step further by indicating that these Vietnam War films establish their ties to the traditional combat film and hint at Hollywood's complicity in the Vietnam disaster. In other words, studying one or more of these films enables students to examine how believing too strongly in their "mass-mediated fantasies" about Vietnam can lead to the same disastrous results depicted in these Vietnam War films. As Bryan notes, the soldiers who went to Vietnam went as innocents and idealists, believing in their John Wayne myths. After a few months in Vietnam, if they survived, they became callous and cynical. Beneath the surface of these films, as with some of the best literature of the Vietnam War, is what Bryan refers to as the horror of the "barely suppressed scream similar to that which pervades the literature of the Holocaust" (1984, 71).

The activity which follows is designed to be used with Stanley Kubrick's *Full Metal Jacket* (1987), but it could easily be modified to be used with one of the other films mentioned in this category. As always, it is important to consider carefully the suitability of a given film for your students. The language and images are strong and may not be appropriate for all students. One possible way around this problem is to assign the film as homework and have students rent the video on their own (with parental approval, of course).

Full Metal Jacket is based on Gustav Hasford's novel, *The Short-Timers*. It tells the story of a young recruit who is inducted into Marine subculture in boot camp, and is then sent to Vietnam as a combat correspondent, where he and an enthusiastic photographer are sent to the front during the 1968 Tet Offensive. They join up with a squad that is part of the force trying to retake the city of Hue from the North Vietnamese Army. The hero and his sidekick experience the horror of the war.

It will take three days to show the film in class. I would suggest starting with an introduction that focuses on the following: (1) background on Kubrick's films and the making of this film (i.e., the fact that, unlike most Vietnam War movies, this one was filmed entirely in England; the screenplay, written by Kubrick, Michael Herr, and Hasford, captures the Vietnam vernacular superbly; etc.); (2) the film takes place during the turning point in the war—the 1968 Tet Offensive; (3) it deals directly with three important themes—the madness of the war, especially in terms of how basic training attempts to turn young men into killing machines; the absurdity of the war; and the warrior-hero myth as passed down through films and television.

It is also worthwhile to discuss the structure of the film. The film can be divided into three acts: Act I focuses on recruit training—how teenagers are turned into killing machines. Viewers see the madness of the war on the home front. In Act II, viewers see how American involvement in Vietnam contributes to the corruption of the Vietnamese, as well as to the growing cynicism of those who are fighting the war. Finally, Act III takes place in Hue, the ancient capital of Vietnam. The Marines are trying to retake the city from the North Vietnamese, and the hero, Joker, is faced with a moral choice (Doherty, 1988). Briefly outlining this structure might help students more easily follow the action and identify themes and issues.

Prior to viewing the film, I lead a class discussion of the warrior-hero in literature, history, and film. I ask students to identify warrior-hero figures they are familiar with, and I list these on the board. Their list often includes people and characters such as Achilles, Odysseus, Robert E. Lee, Ulysses S. Grant, General George Patton, Rambo, Chuck Norris, and Eisenhower, and sometimes even John Wayne. Once the list is complete, we try to generate criteria for defining the warrior-hero. Students often generate two important criteria: (1) the warrior is tested in war, often under fire, and (2) he performs an act of heroism. I tell students to keep these criteria and examples in mind as we view the film and then decide how the warrior-hero is portrayed in the film.

After viewing the film, we discuss how it portrays the warrior-hero. Most students are quick to see that the traditional warrior-hero figure is attacked in the film. They note the fact that Joker constantly makes fun of John Wayne with his "Listen up, Pilgrims. . . ." impersonations. They point out that in the boot camp sequence the drill instructor singles out mass murderer Charles Whitman and Kennedy assassin Lee Harvey Oswald for praise as former Marines. They see that recruit training is designed to turn these young people into killing machines and that when "Private Gomer Pyle" says he "is in a world of shit," kills Sergeant Hartman and then himself, he is the killing machine gone mad.

Students point out that the situation is no better in Vietnam. They see how the Vietnamese are victimized by the Americans. One student notes that when a television camera crew films some grunts for the folks back home, one soldier says, "We'll let the gooks play the Indians." The student recalls that in *Rambo* and *Missing in Action,* the heroes took on the guise of Indian warriors. He wonders if the movie isn't making fun of the Hollywood stereotype of the Vietnam warrior. Students point out other ways that the film debunks the warrior-hero image and point to the final scenes, in which the wounded Vietcong sniper who has wiped out half the squad (itself a debunking of the fantasy of a few Marines killing hordes of enemy soldiers) begs Joker to kill her. Joker attains a kind of purifying transcendence when he kills her and says, "I'm in a world of shit, yes, but I am alive and I am not afraid." He is certainly no John Wayne or Rambo. The final sequence frames the survivors departing Hue at night in a beautiful, bloody haze. They are singing the Mickey Mouse Club theme and not the Marine Corps Hymn, as might be expected in a John Wayne World War II movie. Students see that the film attacks the traditional warrior-hero as portrayed in films and popular literature.

From this discussion we move on to discussing other themes and issues. We tackle the madness of the war, especially as depicted in the first two parts of the film. We also examine the absurdity of the war, and how the film uses satire and black humor to show that absurdity.

As a follow-up, have students write an essay explaining, with evidence from the film, what aspects of the warrior-hero myth are criticized in the film and why. Another possible follow-up is to have students read Hasford's novel *The Short-Timers* and then compare and contrast the novel and the film. Students might focus on the differences between the two endings and on what each says about the Vietnam War, or on why Kubrick changes Hasford's ending in his film.

"Old Kids": Personal Narratives

Myers (1988, 72) points out that "if the Vietnam War novel both extends and revises aspects of traditional American war writing, so the memoir of that war plants and harvests new varieties of personal narrative in the rich earth of its ancestral lands." They not only break new ground, but as Lawson (1988) argues, these nonfiction works have elicited substantial critical praise. Yet, almost none of this impressive canon, which includes oral histories, full-length memoirs, and collected letters, has found its way into the English curriculum.

What is particularly surprising about this situation is that the body of literature dealing with the Vietnam War is very appealing to students and offers nearly unlimited potential for classroom use. Why is this literature so attractive to students? First, it is accessible to nearly all students. As Farrell (1982) points out in arguing that oral histories should be a part of the English curriculum, the speakers of these works establish a confidential, intimate relationship with the reader, in a voice that seems to be speaking directly to them. In addition, Lawson (1988) notes that the voice in these works is one which contains the persuasive power of truth telling that only an eyewitness can claim. More important, she explains that the heart of these works is the adolescent experience. Unlike previous wars, the Vietnam War was America's first war fought by teenagers. The average age of combatants in Vietnam was 19 years as compared with 26 years for the soldier in World War II. The result is that the speakers in these narratives are teenagers much like our students. In addition, because of their youth, many of these young people were not mentally prepared for the carnage and terror that marked the Vietnam experience. As a result, in writing about their experiences, these young people speak of the idealism, loneliness, homesickness, fear, terror, feelings of isolation and abandonment, and finally of betrayal in ways that speak directly to our students. My own students speak of their fascination with these works and how much the speakers seem just like them. In fact, oral historian Mark Baker probably best describes the typical student reaction to these works when he recounts his own reaction to interviewing veterans for his oral history:

There was an aura about the people who were over there. These guys were kids, but they weren't kids. There was something in their eyes that made them absolutely different. I was fascinated, mesmerized by these guys. I couldn't take my eyes off them. There was something very old about them, but I still felt like a kid. (1981, 62)

Many of the activities, units, and courses discussed in the theory section make use of this body of nonfiction. One reason for this is that it lends itself to pedagogical versatility. For example, students might study one of the highly regarded personal memoirs such as Philip Caputo's *A Rumor of War* (1977), Ron Kovic's *Born on the Fourth of July* (1976), Tim O'Brien's *If I Die in a Combat Zone* (1969), or Michael Herr's *Dispatches* (1977). For insight into the Vietnam experience from a woman's perspective, students might read Lynda Van Devanter's *Home before Morning* (1983). Students might also examine one of the excellent oral histories written about the war: Ron Glasser's *365 Days* (1971), Mark Baker's *Nam* (1981), or Al Santoli's *Everything We Had* (1981). For insight into the woman's perspective, students might read Keith Walker's oral history *A Piece of My Heart* (1985). The black experience in Vietnam is explored in Stanley Goff and Robert Sanders's *Brothers: Black Soldiers in the Nam* (1982) and in Wallace Terry's *Bloods: An Oral History of the Vietnam War by Black Veterans* (1984). For insight into the war at home and those who opposed the war, students might study Kim Willenson's *The Bad War: An Oral History of the Vietnam War* (1987). Finally, students might explore the Vietnam experience by studying one of the collections of letters: *Letters from Vietnam* (1967) or *Dear America: Letters Home from Vietnam* (1985). (See the annotated list of resources for a full listing of nonfiction works.)

These works also suggest numerous possibilities for connecting reading and writing. For example, Carter (1989), Cussler (1987), Farrell (1982), Oldham (1986), and others indicate how studying these works helps prepare students for interviewing and writing about veterans and others involved in the Vietnam War. They point out that students learn a variety of research and composing skills when they interview veterans, peace activists, and others about their experiences during the war. Students are able to connect what they are reading with the writing they are doing. Other possible reading/ writing connections include having students compare the experiences of veterans in nonfiction works with those portrayed in fiction, having them compare these nonfiction works with those written from past wars, and having students analyze them as they might any work of literature. These possibilities help students understand how nonfiction writers achieve meaning in their works and the role of nonfiction in literature.

The activities that follow focus on different ways teachers might teach the nonfiction of the Vietnam War and how this literature might be used to connect reading and writing.

"Old Kids" #1: The Adolescent Experience

Lawson's (1988) analysis of the structures and themes of the nonfiction works of the Vietnam War suggests that many of them follow the contours of the *Bildungsroman,* the narrative of education, at the heart of which is the 365-day tour. This overall structure is enhanced by each veteran's desire to tell his story and the need to understand what, exactly, happened to him or her, or to explain, in absolute terms, the effect of having "a lifetime of experience compressed into a year and a half" (Caputo 1977, 4). Lawson says that the process of becoming an "old kid" occurs in five distinct phases which provide the infrastructure for the veterans' narratives. These phases are (1) the mystique of pre-induction, (2) the initiation into boot camp, (3) the dislocation of arrival in Vietnam, (4) the confrontation with mortality in the first firefight, and (5) the phenomenon of coming home, "nineteen-year-old bodies with thirty-five-year-old minds" (Baker 1981, 130).

Such narrative structure also indicates a very effective way to approach teaching this literature. It indicates logical ways to make reading assignments, to organize discussions and other activities, and to explore important structural and thematic elements with students. I have used this structure when my students study the personal narratives and oral histories of veterans. The following questions are from a study guide for the opening section of Mark Baker's *Nam* (1981), which he calls "Initiation." These sample questions get at the specifics of the overall structure of the mystique of pre-induction and the initiation into boot camp, the first two structural elements described by Lawson. See "Lessons and Legacies #1: The Vietnam Experience" (pp. 83–85) for a complete set of questions following Lawson's analysis which, with minor modifications for particular works, could be used for teaching many of the oral histories and personal narratives.

1. Where does the subtitle "Ask Not" come from? Why does Baker use this to introduce this section? Is it meant to be ironic? Why or why not?

2. Where do the people come from who went to Vietnam? What sorts of backgrounds do they come from? How old are most of the speakers?

3. How did they find their way into the military?

4. What seems to have had an effect on many of them in terms of their reasons for going?

5. What was boot camp like for most of them? Do you think it was good training for Vietnam? Why or why not?

6. How are the experiences described by women in this section different from the experiences described by men? How are they alike?

7. How are the experiences described by blacks (and/or other minorities) in this section different from the experiences described by whites? How are they alike?

8. Which of the stories in this section had the most impact on you? Why?

Farrell (1982) describes oral histories as "living literature" (87). These works have such an emotional impact on students that it is important to examine how they achieve their emotional power. In addition, an important aspect of studying these works should involve questions about the veracity of the speakers, the author's selection and arrangement of materials, and the contributions, if any, of these works to the historical record.

These nonfiction works are also rich in the traditional themes explored by nonfiction writers of previous wars. For example, the concepts of heroism and right action are certainly important issues in these works, and teachers may want to focus on these themes in the instruction.

Besides Baker's *Nam*, there are a number of other oral histories and personal narratives that might be read and studied using part or all of Lawson's approach and the additions noted above (see annotated list of resources): Bill Adler's (ed.) *Letters from Vietnam*, Philip Caputo's *A Rumor of War* (1977), Ronald Glasser's *365 Days*, and Al Santoli's *Everything We Had: An Oral History of the Vietnam War by Thirty-three American Soldiers Who Fought It* (1981).

One possible follow-up activity is to have students evaluate how the oral history or personal narrative contributes to the historical record. What insights are added that will help those who study the Vietnam War better understand it? Another possible follow-up is to have students describe one or more aspects of the Vietnam experience, such as the homecoming, using passages from a text they have studied. Finally, one very successful follow-up writing activity is to have students explain the most significant experiences that turn the teenagers into "old kids."

"Old Kids" #2: Independent Reading

Another approach to having students study the nonfiction of the Vietnam War, particularly if they have studied other works of war literature in class, is to have students read one of these works independently. Carter (1989) used this approach in a war unit she taught in a twelfth-grade world literature course. This activity is adapted from her unit.

After students have studied war literature and understand major themes and concepts, have them select a nonfiction work to read on their own. If you have a good school or local library, the librarian might be able to help put together a bibliography from which students select a book of their choice. Another possibility is to put together your own collection for classroom use. Many teachers create collections by purchasing inexpensive paperback books at used bookstores and garage sales.

As students read, they meet in small groups perhaps once a week to discuss what they find in their reading. You might give students questions such as the following to discuss in their groups:

1. What sorts of things influenced these authors and speakers before they went into the military? What generalizations can you make about these influences?

2. How were these individuals initiated into the culture of the military? What were key experiences?

3. How did they arrive in Vietnam? How did each react to the arrival? What conclusions can you make about the typical arrival in Vietnam?

4. How did these people react to their first experience in combat? What realizations did they have?

5. What were their concerns while they were in Vietnam? Did their concerns change? If so, how?

6. How were these people different when they left Vietnam than when they arrived? What changed them?

7. How did these people return from Vietnam? What were their homecomings like? What surprised them?

8. Which of the stories, incidents, or passages had the most impact on you? Why?

In discussing these questions students realize that what they are reading is part of the shared experience of the men and women who served in Vietnam. They come to see how the war affected those who served in Vietnam. You might also have the small groups share their findings with the class. In whole class discussion you might focus on how the experiences are similar to those that other students are reading about. You might explore the implications of this.

Once students have finished their reading and questions, they might give a brief report on the book they have read in their small groups or to the whole class. They might explain why they liked or did not like their book and what they learned about the Vietnam War; they might read a significant passage from the book and explain why it is significant, and discuss why they would or would not recommend that their classmates read the book.

In certain situations teachers may wish to provide a structured study guide for the books students are reading. The example I have provided in the appendix (see p. 172) is keyed to Tim O'Brien's personal memoir *If I Die in a Combat Zone.*

"Old Kids" #3: Guest Speakers

Perhaps the largest untapped resource for bringing the Vietnam War dramatically into the classroom is the guest speaker. A number of teachers who have written about their teaching experiences point to guest speakers as the highlight of their units and courses. For example, Cohen (1988), who teaches high school history, says that Vietnam veterans provided the greatest excitement in his course and motivated his students to do the course work. Wilcox (1988), who teaches a college course on the literature of the Vietnam War, invites veterans, peace activists, and Vietnamese refugees as guest speakers. He argues that they are the most valuable resource a teacher can find because they know something students cannot learn from books, essays, lectures, or films.

However, as Fernekes (1988) points out, designing a sound learning experience around Vietnam veteran classroom speakers can be a complex matter. Veterans differ in their ability and willingness to discuss their experiences and views, and teachers must plan for their visits by developing an adequate interview schedule and helping students learn interviewing skills. Careful planning is the key to ensuring that the experience is worthwhile for everyone involved.

This activity is based on an activity that was originally designed by John Wheeler, who teaches English at Lyons Township

High School in La Grange, Illinois, and on ideas suggested by Cussler (1987). The first task is finding appropriate guest speakers. One of the best sources is probably a local veterans' group. Many of these groups will be more than happy to provide experienced speakers. Some possible groups include the local chapter of the Vietnam Veterans of America, VietNow, Vietnam Veterans against the War, and the local post of the Veterans of Foreign Wars. In addition, many communities have a Veterans' Center or a local Vietnam Veteran Era Outreach Center which may also be willing to provide or help you find an appropriate speaker. My own experience is that there are often Vietnam veterans, peace activists, and others in the community and sometimes in the school who are willing to speak. My own students have often directed me to interesting and appropriate speakers.

Once a speaker has been found and scheduled, the next step is to prepare students for the interview and writing. Inform students that they will be interviewing someone associated with the Vietnam War and will be doing some writing using information gathered in the interview. Cussler (1987) prepares her students for oral history interviews by first reading aloud selections from oral history accounts so that her students can hear the tone and language of the written histories. She follows this by having her students do some writing on what they want to know about the Vietnam War. She then leads a discussion of the questions they generated in this writing and these were used as the basis for formulating actual interview questions. Another technique is to have an in-class brainstorming session for topics, and from these, develop a set of ten to twenty questions the class will ask during the interview.

Spend some time discussing good and bad questions. Steer students away from questions such as, "How many people did you kill?" and "Were you glad to get home from the war?" and "Were you drafted?" and "Did you go to Canada to avoid the draft?" On the other hand, questions such as, "What was your worst experience in Vietnam?" and "What were your feelings about the war?" and "How did you get into the military?" and "Why did you oppose the war?" will usually result in better answers.

Wheeler also has his students develop questions based on the literature of the war they have been studying. Here is a sample of the kind of question he provided as a model for his students:

> In Tim O'Brien's *If I Die in a Combat Zone* the author writes, "Men must know what they do is courageous, they must know

it is right, and that kind of knowledge is wisdom and nothing else" (p. 141). What knowledge about the concept of courage did you discover for yourself as a young soldier in Vietnam? Please describe an action of your own or one you saw that you think was courageous.

This kind of question clearly connects the reading students are doing with this activity. It has the added benefit of encouraging students to do additional thinking about their reading. It connects what they are reading about to the world outside the work of literature. Cussler notes that this exercise is good journalistic training. Students learn how to keep their feelings and ideas to themselves so as not to prejudice the replies they receive with slanted questions.

Some students may need a practice interview session before the actual interview. One way to do this is to have students interview a classmate or the teacher. This helps give students confidence in asking questions and note taking, and they are better prepared for the interview. Students might also evaluate their questions in pairs or small groups to make sure they have good, provocative questions. They should look for good open-ended questions and eliminate or revise yes-no and go-nowhere questions.

With some preparation, the interview itself should go well. If the guest speaker does not object, it is a good idea to audiotape the actual interview. Some students may have difficulty writing everything down. The tape can be played later for students who need to add to their notes.

In the next step of the activity, students experience what professional writers go through in trying to produce a final product. Pass out the assignment, "Writing Based on an Interview" (see appendix, p. 174), which gives students some options for how they might use the material gathered in the interview. Then students begin editing their notes from the interview. They may need some guidance in grouping related ideas, figuring out how to cut out the interview questions, and eliminating extraneous material. They then produce a rough draft of their article, history, or letter. Have students evaluate and revise their drafts in pairs or in small groups before they turn in a final copy.

In conducting the interview and in writing this paper, students learn and apply research and writing skills. Students have gone through the process of researching and writing about an issue and see the importance and necessity of revision. In addition, this activity makes the connection between what they are reading and their writing very clear. What they have read about the Vietnam War comes alive as they become involved in the activity.

"Old Kids" #4: Living History

Although a bit more complex than inviting guest speakers to be interviewed, having students do an oral history project on the Vietnam War can be just as exciting and an even more valuable learning experience. Carter (1989 and 1991), Cussler (1987), Fernekes (1988), and Oldham (1986) have had their students do oral history projects on the Vietnam War. In each case, they report that the results are well worth the effort. Student interest and involvement is very high and the results are often far beyond expectations. Oldham and Cussler find that their students wrote far more than expected; mastered research and writing skills, including mechanics; and produced exceptionally good writing. Carter indicates that the results are "electric" (1991, 292). Fernekes points out that this experience provided his students with important lessons in history. They began to understand the real-life consequences of abstract decisions made in Washington and Hanoi. In addition, he notes that the experience put his students and their concerns at the center of this historical inquiry, "a dynamic alternative to the passive classroom atmosphere engendered by the domination of textbook instruction" (1988, 54).

This activity is based on ideas suggested by the authors cited above and by Farrell (1982). The first step in preparing students for oral history interviews is to have them study some examples from the standpoint of an oral historian instead of a reader of oral history. You might read selections from an oral history to the class and discuss the selections. Another approach is to have students study a few selections in small groups and then discuss their findings. Some selections from Al Santoli's oral history *Everything We Had* (1981) work well for this purpose. They include "Welcome to the War, Boys" (3), "A Puerto Rican Marine" (160–62), and "Life" (163). Hand out the "Oral History Reading Guide" (see appendix, p. 175), which gives students a context for the selections and provides questions for students to answer about the selections. Have the students work on the questions in small groups and then discuss their answers in a whole-class discussion. It is important to make sure students understand how the selections are derived from a set of questions the interviewer had and what kinds of things are important in an oral history.

The next step is to have students learn how to write interview questions. Follow the procedures outlined earlier in "'Old Kids' #3:

Guest Speakers" (pp. 72–75). Also, you might put a bit more emphasis on making sure students have generated enough questions for a one-hour interview.

Students will also need to find someone to interview. The sources outlined in "'Old Kids' #3: Guest Speakers" should provide a good place to start. Students might also be encouraged to interview Vietnamese refugees, peace advocates, conscientious objectors, and former "flower children." Oldham (1986) reports that counselors from the local Vet Center generously provide interviews for students who are unable to find anyone else.

Although students might conduct interviews on their own, the best results seem to occur when students do the interviews in pairs. If there is a shortage of potential interviewees, this team approach can be a lifesaver. In addition, having students conduct the interviews in pairs helps ensure that they will get a good interview. You might assign students to pairs or have them pick someone they want to work with on the project. Students should also secure a tape recorder and tape for the interview. Many students have access to one, but if they do not, many schools will loan them to students.

Students should be given some preparation for conducting the interviews. For example, it is a good idea to have one student in charge of asking the questions and the other in charge of running the tape recorder. Students should be instructed in the following procedures:

1. They should make sure the interviewee permits the interview to be taped.

2. They should be sure the interviewee understands that this is part of a class project and that the transcribed interview will be put in a class book which will be on public display and possibly put in the school or local library.

3. When they arrive for the interview, students should chat informally with the subject to establish rapport before starting the actual interview.

4. They should try to find a place for the interview where they can strategically place the recording equipment and where outside noises are at a minimum.

5. They should not push too hard for certain information during the interview because this might cause a negative reaction on the part of the subject.

6. They should save sensitive questions for the end.

7. They should not be judgmental.

8. At the end of the interview, they should make sure that they have the person's name correctly spelled and the dates and places of his or her service or other pertinent information.

9. They should thank the person for the interview.

Following the interview, the next step is to have the students transcribe their interviews. In transcribing them they should not worry about editing. They should try to type or write them out as nearly verbatim as possible. At this point, however, they may want to eliminate any false starts, stammerings, insignificant repetitions, and offhand comments like, "okay" or "all right."

Once students have transcribed the interview, they are ready for the real work—editing. Here is where they need to focus on eliminating the interview questions, grouping related ideas together, and excluding extraneous material. At this point, they also start focusing on spelling, punctuation, etc. As pairs of students work on editing their interviews, it is often a good idea to have them read their rough drafts to other pairs of students to get response. They might ask the following questions:

1. Is related information grouped together? If not, how could it be reorganized?

2. Has all extraneous material been eliminated? If not, what could be cut out?

3. Is the information organized for impact? If not, how could it be rearranged to have a stronger impact on readers?

When students have finished their histories, they should place them in a binder, which is passed around for all to read. Carter (1991) and Cussler (1987) report that students read these interviews with great interest. In addition, they report that the final products are nothing short of stupendous. The range of reactions, experiences, and viewpoints expressed by veterans and others in these histories is often quite a surprise for students.

Here are a few excerpts from oral histories collected by students:

> When I landed in country I thought it was going to be a war zone. I was going to get off the airplane, they were going to hand me my gun, and "There's the jungle and there's your platoon over there and go join up," but they put you on a bus at the airport and took you to the barracks. They drove by a couple of swimming pools on the way there, and on paved roads. (Cussler 1987, 67)

> We went into a village that was supposed to be pacified—
> that means it's a friendly village. Well, about a ten-year-old
> boy came up to my medic sergeant and my first sergeant and
> handed them a box and walked away. The box went off and
> before that boy reached his next birthday, we all shot him at
> the same time. (Cussler 1987, 67)

> My most memorable experience . . . was this little seven-
> year-old girl I had "adopted." She had lost her mother and
> father . . . and was staying in an orphanage. When the war was
> over I was going to take her home with me. But one night her
> orphanage was bombed and nobody came out alive. That
> experience was real hard for me to swallow for a long time.
> (Carter 1989)

> To go to war or to kill someone or to fight for your country,
> you have to believe in it, and if you don't believe in it, there's
> no way you can do it. I can see the reasoning now, but at the
> time I was too young . . . I really believed I needed to be there.
> (Carter 1989)

These few examples indicate the impact that oral history projects can have on students. Students see the impact that the war has had on those involved, and they gain a sense of the complexity of the issues involved in human terms, something that no textbook or lecture can possibly convey. In addition, students have learned a great deal about writing, and there is the sense of accomplishment that comes with seeing the results of their efforts in the class oral history collection. Projects like this enable students to connect the Vietnam War literature they have read to the world outside of the literature. Most important of all, students no longer see the Vietnam War as some distant historical event that has nothing to do with them; they have touched it, had a part in it, and will not likely forget the lessons they have learned.

"Old Kids" #5: Home Front U.S.A.

In her study of the war's impact on the generation that came of age during the 1960s and 1970s, *Long Time Passing: Vietnam and the Haunted Generation* (1984), Myra MacPherson notes that it is now fashionable to deride the entire generation of nongoers as vain, selfish, and hypocritical six-figure lawyers and executives who have discarded any presumed sixties altruism (701). Yet, the truth is that for the entire Vietnam generation—those who went and those who did not—the war was a cataclysmic time in their adolescence that, to a large extent, shaped the men and women they are today. If our students are going to understand the full impact of the war on the Vietnam generation and on the nation, then it is important that they study literature that examines the effects of the war on the home front.

Besides examining the many fine oral histories and personal narratives that deal with the war at home, one approach that I have used is to have students examine some of the excellent and interesting essays, articles, commentaries, speeches, and other documents that explore the war on the home front. One way to begin is with the "Vietnam War Opinionnaire" (pp. 145–46). Follow the procedures described on pages 29–32. Another way to introduce some of the ideas and concepts students will encounter in these works is to present the class with a list of about ten or so of the more well-known antiwar activists and ask students to tell what they know about each. A good list of people might include some of the following: Jane Fonda, Tom Hayden, Joan Baez, Bob Dylan, Eugene McCarthy, Dr. Martin Luther King, Jr., Allen Ginsberg, Robert Lowell, Timothy Leary, Ron Kovic, Dr. Benjamin Spock, Norman Mailer, Denise Levertov, and Daniel Ellsberg.

After students have told what they know about each of the individuals, ask them what they all have in common. Then ask students to explain or speculate on why they think these people spoke out against the war. Have students note the reasons in their notebooks for later use.

I then have students read James Fallows's essay, "What Did You Do in the Class War, Daddy?" from *The Wounded Generation: America after Vietnam* (see annotated list of resources). The essay describes how Fallows was able to avoid the draft, and he explores how the war has left a heritage of possibilities for class warfare. I lead a class discussion focusing on the issues Fallows raises in his essay. Many students are shocked by the way the draft system made it easy for those with money, power, connections, or knowledge of how the system worked to avoid the draft, while those from the lower classes were drafted in droves. We also discuss the author's surprising proposal that the country needs a draft, but one that is fair to everyone. Many are surprised that a draft avoider would argue for a draft. However, as we examine why Fallows makes this recommendation, students begin to see some of the tragic legacies of the war.

The next step in the activity is to have students read some works on their own. I put students in small groups and give each group a packet of works that they are to read and then prepare in order to give a five- to ten-minute oral report to the class. I give each group a set of questions to guide its reading and help it prepare its report.

Most groups of students receive selections from Woolf and Bagguley's *Authors Take Sides on Vietnam* (1967). This outstanding collection (see annotated list of resources) contains short pieces written by noted authors of the time who responded to two questions: (1) Are you for or against the intervention of the United States in Vietnam? (2) How, in your opinion, should the conflict in Vietnam be resolved? One group of students receives four or five essays by authors who were for the intervention, two or three groups receive essays by authors who were opposed to intervention, and another group receives a packet of essays somewhere in the middle. Authors' pieces that I include are those by Kingsley Amis, William F. Buckley, Jr., Robert Conquest, James A. Michener, W. H. Auden, John Fowles, Robert Graves, Arthur M. Schlesinger, John Updike, Richard Wilbur, Nelson Algren, Nathaniel Benchley, Kay Boyle, Robert Creeley, Richard Eberhart, Lawrence Ferlinghetti, Northrop Frye, Allen Ginsberg, Graham Greene, Joseph Heller, Doris Lessing, Denise Levertov, Arthur Miller, Philip Roth, and Susan Sontag. These distinguished authors have much to say about the war and what they thought at the time should be done about it. Another group of students receives a packet which contains pieces that deal with some of the major riots and protest marches and some of the legacies of the war. These works include Merritt Clifton's "Betrayal" (from *Vietnam Voices*—see annotated list of resources), Sam Brown's "A Legacy of Choices" (from *The Wounded Generation*), an excerpt from Norman Mailer's *The Armies of the Night* (at the Pentagon, October 1967, p. 146—see annotated list of resources), and an excerpt from Ron Kovic's *Born on the Fourth of July* (at the Republican National Convention, 1972, pp. 176–84—see annotated list of resources).

The small groups are given the following questions to help them study and prepare for their oral presentations:

1. What viewpoints on the war are expressed by the authors or others in the selections?

2. What reasons and evidence do they give for their viewpoints? Are their reasons and evidence convincing? Why or why not?

3. What are the immediate effects of the war on individuals and on society? Why?

4. What are the long-term effects (or possible long-term effects) of the war on individuals and on the nation? Why?

5. What are your attitudes toward the viewpoints expressed in your selections? Do you agree with the authors? Why or why not?

Once students have read their selections, met in their small groups to discuss them, and had time to prepare their oral presentations, I set aside two class periods for the giving and discussion of oral presentations. While you may want to have all of the small groups give their presentations without discussion in between, I have found it much more interesting to allow the rest of the class to ask questions after each group gives its presentation. What tends to happen is that groups that have had readings from different perspectives and viewpoints begin to ask some hard questions of the group that has just given a presentation. For example, a student who had read the excerpt from Kovic's book, asked the William F. Buckley, Jr., group, "How can you continue to support the war when the only result is that more and more American boys are sent to Vietnam to be killed and crippled?" A student who had read John Updike's piece asked the Kovic group, "You have talked about American boys being killed and wounded, but what about helping the people of South Vietnam to seek their own political future? How is a village being terrorized by communist troops free to choose?" In a sense, this activity works much like a simulation activity: students take on the roles of the viewpoints expressed in the selections they have been assigned to read.

Once all reports have been given and students have had ample opportunities to raise questions and discuss the issues, I lead a class discussion in which we attempt to draw some conclusions about the issues raised in the readings: What were the major controversies over the war at home? Why were so many people, particularly young people, opposed to the war? What led to the protest marches, riots, and violence across the country over the war? Based on our readings, do you think the U.S. intervention in Vietnam was right or wrong? Why? What are the legacies of the war? This activity encourages students to examine the impact of the war on the home front and to consider the aftermath of the war that continues to shape their lives.

As a follow-up, I sometimes ask students to do some personal-response writing. Which viewpoint presented by the small groups is closest to your own view? Why? Which viewpoint made you angry? Why? Which viewpoint do you disagree with most? Why? Another possible follow-up assignment is to have students read another selection or selections on their own and have students write an analysis of the viewpoint(s) expressed, answering the five guide questions from the small-group activity. They might read other selections from *Authors Take Sides on Vietnam,* or Dr. Martin Luther King, Jr.'s powerful speech, "A Time to Break Silence" (in *Unwinding the Vietnam War*—see annotated list of resources), or "Tet: Three Views" (in *Words of War: An Anthology of Vietnam War Literature* from *The Vietnam Experience* series—see annotated list of resources). This last selection includes three short but very different views from the media on the Tet Offensive of 1968: Columnist William S. White's hawkish view from the *Washington Post,* February 12, 1968; Walter Cronkite's rare personal perspective at the end of his, "Who, What, When, Where, and Why Report from Vietnam" on February 27, 1968; and Art Buchwald's biting satire of the military's optimism in the wake of Tet, "'We have the enemy on the run', says General Custer at Big Horn" from the *Washington Post,* February 6, 1968. These follow-up assignments reinforce what students have learned in the small-group activity and allow them to express their reactions to the selections they have been assigned.

Lessons and Legacies: Teaching Novels

Most teachers who have taught the literature of the Vietnam War—no matter what approach they have taken—report that a rewarding part of their teaching has been the novels. The reason for this is perhaps best expressed by Pratt, who argues, ". . . It is by reading the fiction—an act that takes time, reflection, and empathetic involvement with the human beings who move about in our minds as we feel what the fictional characters experience—that the essential truth of the Vietnam War can best be understood" (1987, 153). In fact, a number of history teachers who teach the war use novels in their units and courses to show "the human side" of the war. They know that Pratt is right: Studying the facts, the political controversies, the military strategies, and the presidential decisions does not convey "the essential truth of the Vietnam War." This is perhaps one of the most important reasons why our students should study the novels that have been written about the war. If our goal is to help our students understand the basic truths of the Vietnam War, they can come to understand them by reading the novels.

The activities that follow illustrate some approaches to teaching different types of Vietnam War novels. These approaches can be easily modified for other novels of a similar type that focus on the war. Other approaches are certainly possible. Some of these were outlined in the theory and research section. There are also other types of novels in addition to those discussed here. For example, Mandel (1988) describes one way to use a teenage novel about the Vietnamese refugee experience.

Lessons and Legacies #1: The Vietnam Experience

In "'Old Kids' #1: The Adolescent Experience," I described how to use Lawson's (1988) analysis of the structure and themes of the nonfiction works of the Vietnam War to teach personal narratives and oral histories. Many Vietnam War novels follow the same basic pattern described by Lawson; that is, they follow the contours of the *Bildungsroman,* or narrative of education, and like their nonfiction counterparts, the heart of these works is the 365-day tour of duty.

However, there are differences between major novels and personal narratives, differences which must be accounted for when teaching these works. One very important difference is that the experience is often much richer than that contained in many of the personal narratives. Pratt's "empathetic involvement" pulls readers along in the characters' experience toward the basic truths of the Vietnam War. In addition, while the heart of these novels might be the 365-day tour of duty (or 395-day tour, in the case of Marines), some of these writers experiment with form and style, which may mean potentially confusing time shifts and/or psychological shifts from reality to fantasy or some other level of consciousness.

Nevertheless, with appropriate modification for particular works, Lawson's five-phase process of becoming an "old kid" is a useful way to begin to organize instruction for teaching a number of Vietnam War novels. These phases, along with some key questions for each, provide the basis for the following overall plan for teaching a Vietnam War novel:

1. **The mystique of preinduction:**

    What are the main character's attitudes toward war?

    Patriotism?

    What is his or her attitude toward the war in Vietnam?

    What are major influences on the main character's attitudes?

    Why does he or she decide to go to war?

2. **The initiation into boot camp—the culture of the military:**

What difficulties does the main character have adjusting to life in the military? Why?

What are significant experiences in recruit training? Why?

How does the main character change as a result of recruit training?

How does recruit training attempt to prepare young people for the war in Vietnam? Is it effective? Why or why not?

3. **The dislocation of arrival in Vietnam—culture shock:**

How does the main character travel to Vietnam?

What are his or her initial experiences upon arrival in country?

How does he or she react to these experiences?

How are the Vietnamese portrayed?

4. **The confrontation with mortality in the first firefight:**

How does the main character react the first time in combat?

What impact does this experience have on the main character? How and why do these concerns change over time?

What are the concerns of the main character and others around him or her?

5. **The phenomenon of coming home:**

How does the main character leave Vietnam?

What is his or her reaction to leaving?

What is the main character's return to the United States like?

How has the main character changed?

What is his or her attitude toward the war?

6. **Putting it together—central meaning:**

What is the author telling readers about the Vietnam War?

What is the author saying about war?

What is the author saying about courage?

Depending on the particular novel, some or all of the following questions may also be important:

7. **Structure:**

How is the novel structured?

How does the structure contribute to the meaning?

8. **Style and literary technique:**

What is the point of view of the novel? Who is telling the story?

Does the point of view change? If so, how?

How does the point of view contribute to the meaning?

What are major literary techniques the author uses?

How do these techniques contribute to the meaning?

Some of the novels that might be taught using this approach include the following: Kent Anderson's *Sympathy for the Devil* (1987); Robert Olen Butler's *The Alleys of Eden* (1981); Philip Caputo's *Indian Country* (1987); Ed Dodge's *Dau: A Novel of Vietnam* (1984); Charles Durden's *No Bugles, No Drums* (1976); Jack Fuller's *Fragments* (1984); Gustav Hasford's *The Short-Timers* (1979); Larry Heinemann's *Close Quarters* (1974); Walter Dean Myers's *Fallen Angels* (1988); James Webb's *Fields of Fire* (1978); and Stephen Wright's *Meditations in Green* (1983). (The annotated list of resources includes these novels and a number of others that might be taught using this approach.)

Lessons and Legacies #2: The Next Generation

An increasing number of writers are beginning to explore the effects of the Vietnam War on the children of the Vietnam generation. Many of these works might be classified as adolescent literature; e.g., Candy Dawson Boyd's *Charlie Pippin* (1987) and Katherine Paterson's *Park's Quest* (1988). The approach described in this activity is based on an idea suggested by Carter (1989) which she has used in teaching Bobbie Ann Mason's excellent novel *In Country*. This novel examines the effects of the war on a seventeen-year-old girl whose father was killed in Vietnam. The approach described here could be easily modified and used to teach any number of works that explore the lingering effects of the war.

This approach centers on examining key issues and themes in the novel. It begins with the classic theme of the hero's quest in finding his or her own identity. Other themes and issues that are important include an examination of the causes of the war; the reasons American boys went to war; the lingering effects of the war; fantasy or romance and reality; the question, "Was the war worth it?"; and reconciliation.

Using these elements as a general guide, teaching the novel might involve the following steps. As students read the novel, have them answer the general "*In Country* by Bobbie Ann Mason: Study

Guide Questions" (see appendix, p. 176). These questions are designed to start students thinking about the issues and themes. Students might meet in small groups once or twice a week to discuss the questions, as well as any others that come up as they read the novel. Once students have finished reading the novel, the teacher leads the class in discussing the issues and themes.

The *"In Country* by Bobbie Ann Mason: Overall Questions" might be used by the teacher to explore themes, issues, and concepts once students have finished the novel. Some of these questions might be used for writing or for evaluation of students' understanding of the novel.

An interesting variation is to assign each small group one of the overall questions to discuss and answer. Then each group prepares and gives an oral presentation to the class on its question. As a follow-up, students might be asked to write on one of the overall questions.

Lessons and Legacies #3: Graphic Representation

Myers (1988) points out that the Vietnam War flashed across American television screens as tight concentrations of violent images in a surreal dreamscape in which language could never hope to keep pace with the cinematic potential of the event. However, Myers notes that the media were never able to connect the images, and they remained "no more than powerful, disquieting snapshots in a new national album, quick cuts in an ongoing newsreel" (3). Vietnam War writers are well aware of the national memory of these images, and the best of them do not fail to confront images such as the American soldier wielding a Zippo lighter against thatched village huts or atrocities like My Lai. In fact, these writers create equally powerful images through language, but unlike the disconnected media "snapshots," these images are connected, and through these connections they create meaning. With this in mind, the following activity is designed to use the powerful images these writers have created.

Another purpose of this activity is to give students an opportunity to demonstrate their understanding of a novel in a manner other than the traditional test or composition. At the same time, no matter what approach the teacher uses in teaching a novel, the following activity encourages students to do some additional thinking about what they have read. It is based on ideas by Judy Cunningham and Joan Brown, Alameda High School, Alameda, California, and by Smagorinsky (1991).

Once the class has finished reading a novel, have students select one of the assignments in "Vietnam War Novel: Images of War" (see appendix, p. 178). When the graphic representations are due, the teacher might have students show and explain them in small groups or to the whole class. Then they can be displayed in the classroom for all to see.

Besides being fun, this activity gives students who have difficulties with tests or compositions a chance to demonstrate their understanding of the novel the class has studied. It also often results in some very creative and insightful work. Students are typically very interested in the graphic representations produced by other students. As they examine the work produced by their peers, it is not uncommon for students to have additional insights and make new connections between theme and structure or character development.

"Some Truths": Character Analysis in a Novel

After years of my teaching the literature of the Vietnam War, it is my students who continually remind me of a simple truth about this literature, and indeed all literature, if it is worth studying—it is the human beings, the characters, that hold their interest, fascinate them, and evoke their empathy, and it is through the characters that they come to understand some truths about the Vietnam War. The reason for this is perhaps best stated by Baker (1981), who writes:

> War poses all the hard philosophical questions about life and death and morality and demands immediate answers. The abstractions of scholarly debate become the very concrete matters of survival. In one short year, Vietnam took the measure of a man and of the culture that put him there. War strips away the thin veneer applied slap-dash by the institutions of society and shows Man for exactly what he is. We must listen closely to the men and women who became both the victims and the perpetrators of the war, if we want to learn something real about this particular conflict, something real about the human spirit, something real about ourselves." (1981, *xvi*)

The activities in this section are based on the idea that one of the most effective ways we can help our students understand the Vietnam War, as well as the literature of the war, is by focusing instruction on the characters, or, in other words, by having our students "listen closely" to the voices of those who fought in the war. However, hearing what characters have to say is not all that easy for most students because they must make inferences about characters' experiences in order to understand what authors are saying about the war. Therefore, these activities are designed to be taught in a sequence that engages students in an interpretive problem, helps them make complex interpretations, and enables them to transform their conclusions into effective literary analysis. In other words, they are designed to help students come to a sophisticated understanding of the essential truths an author attempts to convey through characters and to transform that understanding into an effective literary analysis essay.

While these activities are designed to be used with James Webb's *Fields of Fire* (1978), they can easily be modified so that they can be used with many other novels such as John M. Del Vecchio's *The 13th Valley* (1982), Jack Fuller's *Fragments* (1984), Larry Heinemann's *Close Quarters* (1974), William Turner Huggett's *Body Count* (1982), and Tim O'Brien's *Going after Cacciato* (1979). In addition, with some modification, this sequence of activities works very well with many short stories, plays, personal narratives, and films.

It is also important to mention why I use and recommend Webb's *Fields of Fire* for classroom use rather than one of the other equally fine novels. First, as Pratt (1987) notes in his "Bibliographic Commentary "'From the Fiction, Some Truths,'" ". . . It is one of the few novels that moves realistically from the home scene (1968–69) to Vietnam and back home again (1970)" (146). In other words, Webb provides a clear historical context that is very helpful to readers, particularly students who know very little about the war, and the novel takes place during a pivotal time period in the war, from the Tet Offensive through the invasion of Cambodia.

In addition, as Herzog (1980) argues in a review of major Vietnam War literature, one of "the book's strengths is its realism." Without the elaborate plot structures of some other major novels, "Webb can concentrate on developing interesting and relevant characters" (692). For teaching purposes, this means that the novel is accessible, and it offers an unusual opportunity for examining the effects of the war on various characters. This is important because as students discover in reading the novel and in analyzing the characters, there is no simple truth about Vietnam. The novel demands that students reconsider oversimplified myths and images of the war.

I begin this sequence of activities with the "Vietnam War Opinionnaire" (see "First Contact #1: Vietnam War Opinionnaire," pp. 29) as a means of introducing and preparing students for themes and some of the interpretive problems they will encounter in their reading. The next activity, "Character Analysis," helps students make inferences regarding the three main characters prior to and up through their first few weeks in Vietnam. In addition, students orally practice argumentation skills that are essential in written discourse involving literary analysis. In a follow-up activity, students evaluate interpretive conclusions and evidence from the "Character Analysis." When students have finished the novel, they reconsider the three major characters in light of their experiences in Vietnam and at home in the "Discovering Essential Truths" activity. They also practice and refine skills involved in writing a character analysis. This activity prepares them for a final writing assignment. "Planning and Composing" asks students to pull together all that they have learned and practiced in writing a character analysis of one of the three major characters. Before students turn in a final composition, they evaluate their peers' rough drafts as a final check, and once compositions are returned, students share their writing with other students.

"Some Truths" #1: Character Analysis

This activity is designed to help students analyze a character's values, to help them delve into a personality and discover those things that motivate a character, to help them move beyond a superficial reading and response to a work of literature. The activity is adapted from one originally developed by Kahn, Walter, and Johannessen (1984).

Students are given a list of twenty-two values (see "Character Analysis" handout in appendix, p. 180) which they rank for a particular character. They rank the character's most important and least important values early in the novel (and in a later activity, at or near the end of the work). Making these rankings requires students to make complex inferences. They must consider and weigh many possibilities. In making their choices, and in subsequent steps in the activity in which they debate with peers in small-group and whole-class discussions, students refine their initial interpretations and practice supporting and explaining their conclusions with evidence from the novel.

I use this activity to focus on the three major characters in the novel: Snake, Hodges, and Senator (Goodrich). Fortunately, Webb structures his novel so that the teacher can have students work on what each character's values are early in the work (the first column), either one or two at a time, as he introduces each character or after students have read the first hundred and twenty pages or so. Webb introduces the character of Snake first, then Hodges, followed by Senator.

I like to do the activity after the first two characters have been introduced. Once students have read far enough into the novel, I pass out the "Character Analysis" sheet (two per student). I go over the definitions of any difficult terms and have students spend a few minutes ranking the values for Snake and Hodges. Then I put students in small groups and have them try to reach a consensus on their rankings.

As students discuss their rankings, they make some interesting discoveries about these characters. For example, they quickly learn that each character is motivated by very different values. Students also quickly discover that others in their groups have somewhat different rankings. For example, some students rank "tradition" as Hodges's most important value because his primary reason for joining the Marines and going to Vietnam is based on the fact that he grew up in a strong Southern warrior culture. In fact, students point to his name, "Robert E. Lee," as evidence of his ties to the warrior culture. In addition, students argue that the Hodges family has a long history of fighting in all of America's wars. However, other students argue that his most important value is "recognition." Students point to his actions when he first takes over the platoon and in his first night ambush as evidence that he wants the men in the platoon to recognize him as an excellent platoon commander.

In discussing their rankings, students find specific and concrete ways to talk about the actions and motives of a character. As students debate possible values, they reach a fuller understanding of each character.

Once students reach a consensus in their small groups, I have them debate their ideas in a whole-class discussion. I usually begin by writing the characters' names on the board and under each name writing, "1. _____, 2. _____, 3. _____," for writing in possible top values, and writing, "20. _____, 21. _____, 22. _____," for possible bottom values. I then go from group to group and ask for each one's top three and bottom three values. As the groups report, I write in their rankings. While many of the groups have similar values in the top and bottom three rankings, they never completely agree on any of the rankings.

We then begin debating their ideas in a whole-class discussion. As the groups compare answers and discuss why they ranked a character's values the way they did, the discussion is at a high level because of their previous work. One of the most exciting aspects of the activity is that in order to argue that one value is more important than another, students must look to the text in order to support their interpretations.

Sometimes the discussion concludes with most or all students agreeing on rankings for one or both characters. More often than not, however, there is still some disagreement. This disagreement provides an excellent opportunity for students to do a short follow-up writing assignment in which they explain why one value such as "self-respect" is more or less important than another value such as "power" or "skill" for the character of Snake.

The next step in the activity is to have students rank the values for the third major character, Senator. I usually have students do this on their own and then have them meet in their small groups to discuss their rankings. Once the groups have finished their rankings, I have them debate their findings in a whole-class discussion. Once again, the small-group and whole-class discussions are usually at a high level. The activity seems to provide a useful framework for students to think about and discuss the psychological makeup of characters and those characteristics that motivate actions. Doing this activity early in the novel provides students with a basis for talking about characters and their development as students read the novel. My experience has been that as a result of this early work, the level of student analysis as they read, and in subsequent discussions, is much higher. When all three characters have been discussed, I tell students to retain their "Character Analysis" sheets for use in conjunction with later activities.

One variation on the procedure outlined above is to have students do the "Character Analysis" as each character is introduced. It is important, however, to have students discuss their rankings in small groups and then again in whole-class discussions for at least two of the characters. It is in the discussions that students refine their initial conclusions and ultimately arrive at a sophisticated understanding of each character.

"Some Truths" #2: Supporting Interpretations

This activity has two purposes: (1) to reinforce analytical skills students learned in the previous activity and (2) to help students learn how to translate their interpretations of character into written discourse. Building on the ideas about the characters' values discussed in the previous activity, it is designed to follow reading and discussion up through chapter 27, or a little over halfway through the novel. A similar format can be used in dealing with many different works of literature. The activity is adapted from Kahn, Walter, and Johannessen (1984).

Many students do not understand what is meant when they are asked to give specific evidence or when they are asked to explain how a specific piece of evidence supports a conclusion. They often think that a statement like "Hodges was told about his warrior ancestors" is good supporting evidence to show that "tradition" is his most important value. In addition, when students do present evidence, they assume that the evidence "speaks for itself." This activity is designed to help students learn how to use specific quotations and details from a literary work as supporting evidence for their conclusions.

Begin by handing out "Supporting Interpretations" (see appendix, p. 181), directing students to complete part A. While this activity can be done individually by students, it usually works best in small, heterogeneous groups of three to five students so that group members can help each other and thus refine their answers.

After students have completed the assignment, assemble the class to discuss findings. Students begin to understand what makes good evidence as they present their ideas to the class and get responses from their peers. One group may say that "Senator says that it is stupid to do something for somebody else because all that it means is that you end up dying for another fool who is dying for you." Another group replies, "When does that happen? You need to tell more about it." The first group is then forced to be more specific as it relates the situation in which Snake tells Senator that he only cares about himself and Senator responds by explaining how ridiculous it is to help someone when all you are doing is dying for each other. Students also see that a piece of evidence might be very specific (statement 3), but if it has nothing to do with the stated interpretation, it is not at all persuasive. In discussing which evidence is most specific and persuasive and how to make weak evidence more specific and persuasive, students begin to see what will be necessary to support an interpretation.

Students should next work on part B. In this step of the activity students are asked to write explanations for evidence that supports another possible conclusion about Senator's most important value in the first part of the novel. Lead a class discussion in which they present their explanations for the class to evaluate. Effective explanations will clearly and logically link the evidence to the overall interpretation. Since the evidence listed could be interpreted in several ways, students begin to understand why the evidence alone does not completely support their conclusions. For example, the first piece of evidence requires that students explain how refusing to fire at a group of fleeing enemy soldiers dressed as women and children supports the idea that Senator values "morality." Without the explanation, the connection may not be clear.

As the class evaluates explanations, students also see why an explanation like "This example shows that Senator values morality" is inadequate. Students realize that they need to explain *how* their evidence supports a conclusion. This part of the activity also helps students understand how to incorporate evidence into a written text. As we discuss each example, I have the class examine how the context for each piece of evidence is provided. We then compare these to what is actually in the text. Students see the importance of providing a context for evidence and how this evidence and explanation might be incorporated into a paragraph of written discourse.

As a follow-up writing practice, refer students back to the "Character Analysis" sheets they completed on the characters of Hodges and Snake, and have them write a paragraph indicating their interpretation of what one of these characters values most prior to coming to Vietnam and during his first few months in Vietnam or in the first part of the novel. I ask them to include at least two pieces of evidence and explain how each piece of evidence illustrates what the character values most.

"Some Truths" #3: Discovering Essential Truths

Once students have finished reading the novel, I have them do the "Character Analysis" activity again (see appendix, p. 180) for one or more of the three main characters. This time they rank the character's values at or near the end of the novel. I have students discuss their rankings in small groups and follow this with a whole-class discussion of what the groups have found. One of the interesting discoveries they make involves the character of Senator. When they do the activity early in the novel, many students rank "health," or his own personal survival, as one of Senator's top values and "loyalty" as one of his least important values. Students argue that Senator was not concerned about the other men in the squad, and that his most important motivating drive was saving his own skin. However, when they rank his values at the end of the novel, after he has returned from Vietnam, students often put "loyalty" as one of his most important values and "health" as one of his least important values. As the class discusses the reasons for this change, students discover how and why Senator has been deeply affected by his experiences in the war.

The connections students make in analyzing how the characters have or have not changed often leads to discussions of other important themes and issues in the novel. For example, students note that upon his return home, Senator faced civilians' hostile attitudes, misconceptions about the war, or simple indifference. They see that Senator had to confront his own feelings about the war and act upon his emotions. They also end up comparing Senator's situation and reaction to that of a second returning Marine, Staff Sergeant Gilliland. Unlike Senator, who is haunted by what happened in Vietnam, Gilliland's reaction is quite different. He does his best to ignore those he confronts and tries to get on with his life. Students are often shocked and even angered at the treatment these returning soldiers experienced at the hands of their fellow Americans. One of my students remarked, "People treat them like they are from outer space or something." Webb's handling of the Vietnam veterans' coming home is powerful and perhaps one of the distinctive aspects of the novel. It is through the characters that students are able to understand truths about human nature and the realities of the Vietnam War.

"Some Truths" #4: Planning and Composing

In previous activities, students have practiced the skills involved in analyzing a character and convincing others of their conclusions. At this point students should be ready for a more independent activity in which they must apply what they have learned.

Hand out the "Composition Planning Sheet" (see appendix, p. 183). It contains an assignment that asks students to select one of the main characters in the novel—Hodges, Snake, or Senator—and write a composition in which they explain how the character's values change and why. It suggests that their thesis might focus on the character's top value at the beginning of the novel, his top value at the end, and the reasons for the change in values.

The planning sheet asks students to do the "Character Analysis" (see appendix, p. 180) for the character they are going to write about (if they have not already done it in the previous activity). Once students determine the character's values at the beginning and at or near the end of the novel, they fill out the planning sheet. The sheet is set up to help students find evidence and provide reasoning to support their analysis of the character's values. In addition, the sheet helps students find evidence and develop reasoning that will explain the causes of the character's change in values.

This last point is important in terms of how the sequence of activities helps students come to a more sophisticated understanding of the impact of the war on those who went to Vietnam. Without this kind of analysis of how the war changed these characters, students look at the character of Senator at the end of the novel and want to say something like "Well, look what Vietnam did to him." The problem with this response is that it fails to deal with the real question: What was it about his experiences in Vietnam that brought about these dramatic changes in Senator? In fact, in analyzing this character, students must confront the reality that Senator has mixed feelings about the war. Students discover that Senator hated the war and feels guilty about the fact that he survived while others did not, but they also realize that he misses the action and togetherness of combat and feels a sense of pride in his newfound self-awareness and maturity gained in combat.

Once students have completed the planning sheet, have them write their compositions; or if you think they need a bit more help before they begin writing, you might have them meet in small groups to evaluate planning sheets before they write their papers.

"Some Truths" #5: Revising and Sharing

On the day that students bring their rough drafts to class, divide them into small groups to evaluate each other's papers. In groups, each student reads his or her paper aloud, and the other group members work together to fill out the "Check Sheet" (see appendix, p. 185) about the composition. The group should discuss each paper with the writer and explain reasons for the comments selected. After the group discussions, the check sheets and papers should be given to the writers so they can make revisions.

As a final step in the activity, students might share their revised compositions with other students. They might read them aloud in small groups or to the whole class. Having students share their compositions underscores the idea that writing is the act of communicating ideas to an audience. It can also be an opportunity for students to reexamine their conclusions about the novel. After students have shared their compositions, lead a class discussion focusing on what new ideas or insights they learned from hearing other students' essays, and how what they learned changed or gave further support to their interpretations of the novel.

The following student composition, "Memories of Days Gone By," is an example of the kind of composition students write. The essay shows a sophisticated analysis of the character of Senator and an effective use of evidence to support the student's viewpoint. It is important to note that this student's class did not do the "Supporting Interpretations" activity described earlier, which focuses on the character of Senator. Instead, it did a similar activity that focused on the character of Hodges.

This student essay illustrates that the literature of the Vietnam War does have a place in the English classroom. After students have completed a sequence of activities like that described in this section, they have a much more sophisticated understanding of the Vietnam War and the literature dealing with the war. War, too, is no longer a vague abstraction, a China-Beach-Party myth or a Ramboesque, shoot-'em-up image, but rather a very real possibility, with consequences that they had never before imagined.

Janet T.
Images of War
English 160

Memories of Days Gone By

In James Webb's *Fields of Fire,* the character of Will Goodrich, nicknamed "Senator," is a soldier who throughout his tour of duty in Vietnam is unable to understand or rationalize his feelings concerning the war and the men he serves with. Early in the novel, Senator's most important value is morality, regardless of the circumstances. By the end, however, it is loyalty that becomes most meaningful to him. There are several reasons for this change, but the primary cause is the death of New Mac, which Senator feels personally responsible for.

Early in the novel, and throughout his time in Vietnam, Senator values morality above all other things. For example, he feels compassion for the "sickly and unwashed" children he sees in the village of Phu Phong (4) (90). While at the village, refilling his canteen at a well, he turns to one of his comrades and says, "I just can't help feeling sorry for them. . . . None of this is *their* fault" (90–91). He is reminded by his companion that "None of this is *our* fault, either" (91). Still he feels morally responsible, somehow, for their wretched condition. It's just not right that these children should be so wronged, according to Senator. Much later in the novel, while within the safety of a "two-day perimeter" (171), he sees another group of village children, "staring numbly at him like four dirty, stolid statues. He felt like helping them" (174). Senator makes a deal with the children—if they help him wash himself at the village well, he will wash them and give them food. He does this even though "he was under orders not to give food to civilians" because it would likely end up aiding the enemy. Senator defies the order, with the excuse that "he didn't care anymore" (174). In reality, Senator defies the order because he feels it is his moral duty to aid these helpless children. His morality is the driving force behind his action.

Senator's sense of morality is so strong that it prevents him from performing his duty as a soldier. For example, a couple of months after Senator accidentally wounds and nearly kills a village woman, Hodges orders him to shoot at what appear to be villagers fleeing toward No-Name Ridge, Senator replies, "Those are kids, Lieutenant. Kids and mamasans" (157). He cannot accept the idea that they may be the enemy. He fires his "weapon perfunctorily in the general direction of the fleeing mob. [He thinks,] What the hell. He can court-martial me for not shooting, but he can't court-martial me for being a lousy shot" (157). Senator's strong moral beliefs coupled with his naivete regarding the reality of the situation—the fleeing figures are enemy soldiers disguised as villagers—prevent him from performing his duty as a soldier.

What Senator does after the incident on Go Noi Island is the most telling example of the importance he places on morality. When the company returns to An Hoa (the rear), Senator decides that he must report the incident to the Regimental Legal Officer. Members of Senator's squad had killed two Viet Cong suspects who may have been responsible for or at least involved in the murders of Baby Cakes and Ogre. Senator believes the killings were murder. As he walks to the legal office, he thinks about "the killings" and concludes,

> But if I ignore this, how can I ever face myself, much less anyone else? . . . We can't play God. We can't administer street justice—what the hell: bush justice—to every Vietnamese who pisses us off (335).

In other words, Senator's strong sense of morality will not permit him to "ignore" the killings. As he reasons,

> . . . there's no way to justify murder. The rules say kill, O.K. but when the rules say stop, you've got to stop. We're not God. We're not barbarians (335).

Here again, it is Senator's strong sense of morality that causes him to come forward and also prevents him from seeing that what happened on Go Noi Island was probably not murder, or as the legal officer says, "It's not exactly your clear-cut case" (340).

It is evident that Senator considers morality his most important value throughout his tour in Vietnam. It is not until he returns home that any change in values is evident. It becomes apparent that what he has come to value most is loyalty—loyalty to the memory of the men he served with in the bush—and that which he valued least while in Vietnam. For example, shortly after he gets out of the hospital, Senator has a talk with his father about Vietnam and tells him,

> I have some good memories. I have some *bad* memories. But I do have some good ones. I even miss it, in a way (393).

This is a surprising comment from a man who once put jelly on his "gook-sores" in the hope that they would get infected and he would get sent to the rear and away from the men in his platoon who lacked his "maturity" and "moral principles" (335). What "good" memories could Senator possibly have about Vietnam and what could he possibly "miss" even a little bit? The narrator explains:

> Surprisingly, he found himself most often inside the pages of his Vietnam scrap book. He had put it together in the hospital, spending whole dull days sorting out the stacks of Instamatic photos, placing them in their proper chronology, identifying grinning, youthful faces and writing names underneath the photos. . . . And the friends. Yes, friends . . . . And on every page he saw himself. Or what he used to be. . . . And them. He would gaze at the pictures of them noting all the penned in names of dead men, lamenting their loss and so lamenting himself (394).

It is evident here that this is a changed Goodrich. He no longer considers himself morally superior to the men he served with; instead, he sees himself as being one of them and he thinks of them as his "friends."

Senator is able to show his loyalty to the men he served with at an anti-war rally on the campus of Harvard University. Senator is asked to speak to a large crowd and tell them, "how [bad] it was in the Nam. How senseless the killings were. The whole immorality bit" (406). When Senator arrives at the rally, he sees the Viet Cong flag raised and hears the crowd chanting, "HO! HO! HO CHI MINH! THE N.L.F. IS GONNA WIN!" (406) Standing "isolated on the stage," the chanting seems to mock the memory of those Senator left behind in Vietnam, and he thinks,

> And a thousand corpses rotted in Arizona.
> And a hundred ghosts increased his haunted agony.
> Snake, Baby Cakes and Hodges, all the others peered down from uneasy, wasted rest and called upon the Senator to Set The Bastards Straight. And those others, Bagger, Cannonball, and Cat Man, now wronged by a culture gap that overrode any hint of generational divide (406).

For Senator this is his moment of truth. The dead and wounded he served with are demanding that he tell the truth about the war. Senator knew what the students wanted to hear and what he was expected to say, but his shouted response reveals that Senator is now motivated by loyalty rather than a misguided sense of morality that simply did not work in the bush of Vietnam:

> "... HOW MANY OF YOU ARE GOING TO GET HURT IN VIETNAM? I DIDN'T SEE ANY OF YOU IN VIETNAM. I SAW DUDES, MAN. DUDES. AND TRUCK DRIVERS AND COAL MINERS AND FARMERS. I DIDN'T SEE YOU. WHERE WERE YOU? FLUNKING YOUR DRAFT PHYSI-CALS? WHAT DO YOU CARE IF IT ENDS? YOU WON'T GET HURT" (409).

Senator's verbal assault on the values of the college students at the anti-war rally indicates that he is now motivated by loyalty to the memory of the men he served with in Vietnam. The microphone was ripped out of his hands, and as he left the speaker's platform, passing angry and hostile stares, he smiled and thought, "Snake would have loved it, would have grooved on the whole thing. Senator, he would have said, you finally grew some balls" (410). This was Senator's way of repaying the loyalty that was given to him without question while he was in Vietnam.

Senator's change in values was brought about mostly by the killing of New Mac which Senator feels was his fault. Senator recounts the story of New Mac's death to the two students who ask him to speak at the anti-war rally. He tells them,

> A little babysan sucked me right out into the open so the NVA could start an ambush. I was a team leader. I had a kid who was going to shoot her. I knocked his rifle down. Just in time to see him shot in the face. Do you know how it feels to know you caused that. I'll see his face staring at that babysan for the rest of my life. . . . If I hadn't had the shit blown out of me, it would have given me great pleasure to hunt that little girl down and blow her away (407).

This is a very different Senator speaking than the one who refused to fire on fleeing figures because they looked like innocent villagers (157). Senator is admitting that it was his sense of morality that resulted in the death of New Mac. More importantly, he now realizes what the other men knew all along: that his loyalty belonged to those he served with, to those who were loyal to him. By saying that he would have hunted the little girl down and killed her, Senator is indicating that it is this incident more than anything else that brought about his change in values.

Senator entered the war with a strong sense of right and wrong, which he tries to apply to what he sees and experiences in Vietnam. His sense of morality blocks his ability to be an effective soldier, motivates him to turn in Snake and the guys for what he thinks is a case of murder, and even causes him to make a critical mistake in combat that results in the death of New Mac. As a result of this incident, Senator comes to realize the true meaning of loyalty. He learns to value loyalty to the men he served with, and at the anti-war rally he repays some of the loyalty the men showed to him.

Selected and Annotated Resources for Classroom Use

"In the end, of course, a true war story is never about war. It's about the special way that dawn spreads out on a river when you know you must cross the river and march into the mountains and do things you are afraid to do. It's about love and memory. It's about sorrow. It's about sisters who never write back and people who never listen."

—Tim O'Brien, "How to Tell a True War Story"

There is a large and growing body of Vietnam War literature and films. Deciding what to teach from among this literature involves some problems which I try to address in the list of selected resources. For those who want to know more about the war itself—the history, politics, and some of the issues—I have included a list of general nonfiction for teachers. For those who are concerned about the quality of the literature, I have included works that critical studies point to as the best to come out of the war. Availability is another very real concern many teachers may have, and I have tried to address this problem by including works that are, for the most part, fairly easy to obtain, and whenever possible, I have indicated alternative sources for particular works. Many teachers want to know which works are best for a particular group of students. To help them, I have included works that are appropriate and effective for students from elementary through undergraduate classes. Many of the texts and films I have used myself; others have been recommended to me by teachers; and still others have been recommended by scholars and teachers in published sources. Texts and films that are more difficult are followed by a [_]. I have also indicated a recommended age range for some texts and films, and those followed by a [+] are especially recommended for classroom use. Works followed by a [-] contain particularly violent language or images.

I have drawn on a number of sources in putting together this annotated list of resources. Some of the entries are derived from Carter (1989 and 1991), Christie (1989), Farish (1988), Paris (1987), and

Wittman (1989), as well as the many course bibliographies, course descriptions, and recommendations that teachers have shared with me over the years.

I have tried to organize the list of resources in a way that would make it easy to use. The entries are listed under the following headings and in the following order:

1. General Nonfiction Recommended for Teachers
2. Personal Narratives, Oral Histories
3. Novels
4. Drama
5. Poetry
6. Short Stories
7. Short Story Collections
8. Anthologies
9. Photography/Art Collections
10. Films

The short stories section requires some explanation. In that section, I have listed individual short stories. Each entry notes the original source of the story, as well as alternative sources. If the alternative source is an anthology or short story collection that is listed in this bibliography, then I have just indicated the title of the work. However, if the alternative source is not listed elsewhere in this bibliography, then I have provided complete bibliographic information.

General Nonfiction Recommended for Teachers

Baskir, Lawrence M., and William A. Strauss. *Chance and Circumstance: The Draft, the War, and the Vietnam Generation.* New York: Knopf, 1978.

> A study of the Vietnam generation and how the war affected the 53 million Americans who came of draft age between 1964 and 1973. The authors discuss avoiders, evaders, deserters, and exiles. Personal accounts of experiences are found throughout the book, some of which are very appropriate for classroom use. The charts and statistics provide an excellent breakdown of just what segment of the population actually fought the war.

Boettcher, Thomas D. *Vietnam: The Valor and the Sorrow.* Boston: Little, Brown, 1985.

The author served as an Air Force liaison to the press in Vietnam. His is a popular history of the war based on his experiences.

Broughton, Jack. *Going Downtown: The War against Hanoi and Washington.* New York: Orion, 1988.

Broughton was an Air Force pilot who presents the story of the bombing campaign waged against North Vietnam. The book contains an introduction by Tom Wolfe and includes photographs.

Buter, David. *The Fall of Saigon: Scenes from the Sudden End of a Long War.* New York: Dell, 1985.

The author was a reporter in Vietnam, and his book describes the events leading up to the fall of Saigon and a minute-by-minute description of the fall itself.

Emerson, Gloria. *Winners and Losers: Battles, Retreats, Gains, Losses and Ruins from the Vietnam War.* New York: Random House, 1976.

A correspondent for the *New York Times* during the war, Emerson discusses the effect of the war on both America and Vietnam as well as individuals on both sides. The book utilizes observations and interviews with POWs, veterans, antiwar demonstrators, deserters, etc.

FitzGerald, Frances. *Fire in the Lake: The Vietnamese and the Americans in Vietnam.* New York: Vintage, 1972.

A good history of U.S. involvement in Vietnam. Many regard it as one of the best. It won the Pulitzer Prize and National Book Award.

Karnow, Stanley. *Vietnam: A History.* New York: Penguin, 1984.

This history is considered by many to be *the* history book on U.S. involvement in Vietnam. A very readable history of the war, it was the basis for the PBS television series.

Lifton, Robert J. *Home from the War: Vietnam Veterans—Neither Victims nor Executioners.* New York: Simon & Schuster, 1973.

This is a psychological study of the soldier in Vietnam and at home. It focuses on those involved in atrocities like My Lai. One conclusion the author makes is that Vietnam veterans are more alienated than veterans of other wars.

McPherson, Myra. *Long Time Passing: Vietnam and the Haunted Generation.* Garden City, N.Y.: Doubleday, 1984.

The author interviewed 500 men and women to assess the impact of the war on the generation that came of age during the 1960s and 1970s. McPherson covers a number of important topics and emphasizes the human cost of the war.

Manning, Robert, ed. *The Vietnam Experience Series.* Boston: Boston Publishing Company, 1981–88.

Manning is the editor in chief of this twenty-five volume series, which provides a very extensive overview of the war.

Millett, Allan R., ed. *A Short History of the Vietnam War.* Bloomington: Indiana University Press, 1978.

A good account of the war and very readable.

Polner, Murray. *No Victory Parades: The Return of the Vietnam Veteran.* New York: Holt, Rinehart & Winston, 1971.

The author interviewed over 200 veterans. This is an interesting study of the impact of the war on those who fought.

Pratt, John Clark. *Vietnam Voices: Perspectives on the War Years, 1941–1982.* New York: Viking, 1984.

Pratt is a retired lieutenant colonel, English professor, and a Vietnam War archivist. His book is a history and personal narrative with many interviews, official documents, poems, and excerpts from personal narratives and novels. He attempts to include all points of view.

Personal Narratives, Oral Histories

Adler, Bill, ed. *Letters from Vietnam.* New York: Dutton, 1967.

A collection of letters home compiled prior to the end of the war. There are letters from soldiers, parents, nurses, volunteers working with Vietnamese peasants, Red Cross workers, U.S. civilian personnel, and Vietnamese citizens.

Anderson, Charles R. *Vietnam: The Other War.* San Rafael, Calif.: Presidio Press, 1982.

When Anderson arrived in Vietnam in 1968, he was assigned to "service and support" in "the rear" near Da Nang, where he served the first half of his tour of duty. He details what life was like here and all of the diversions from standard operating procedure needed to make things work. An interesting and often entertaining examination of the soldier's life away from the battlefield. Selections from this book have been anthologized in *Touring Nam: The Vietnam War Reader.* [–]

Baker, Mark. *Nam: The Vietnam War in the Words of the Men and Women Who Fought There.* New York: Morrow, 1981.

Wittman (1989) describes this as "a very powerful, honest, and touchingly written book." It is certainly one of the classics of Vietnam literature. Baker interviewed both men and women, officers, enlisted men of all kinds, prowar and antiwar veterans. He asked them, "What was Vietnam really like?" The introduction is effective, and the interviews are organized around themes, which allows for useful comparison with other literature. [+/–]

Beesley, Stanley W. *Vietnam: The Heartland Remembers.* Norman: University of Oklahoma Press, 1987.

A well-written, poignant oral history of thirty-three Oklahomans who speak "for heartland America." All of those interviewed were involved in the war, either as soldiers or as family members who waited. This is the story of ordinary people forced into extraordinary circumstances. [–]

Brandon, Heather. *Casualties: Death in Vietnam, Anguish and Survival in America.* New York: St. Martin's, 1984.

An interesting and different oral history. The author focuses on those who suffered at home. Thirty-seven survivors tell of their hope, fear, mourning, their changing feelings toward the war, and their efforts at healing. These are the stories of the mothers, fathers, sisters, brothers, children, lovers, wives, friends, and even grandparents of soldiers who died in Vietnam. The book includes all classes and ethnic groups. The author is a Vietnam veteran counselor. The book really tugs at your heart and shows the effects of war on those at home. [+]

Broyles, William. *Brothers in Arms: A Journey from War to Peace.* New York: Knopf, 1986.

The author of this account served as a Marine lieutenant in Vietnam, leading a platoon near Da Nang in 1969. Later, he became editor in chief of *Newsweek,* a job he left in 1984 to return to Vietnam to discover the meaning of the war. His observations are often moving.

Bryan, C.D.B. *Friendly Fire.* New York: Putnam, 1976.

One of the early Vietnam classics, Bryan's book chronicles the 1970 death of Sergeant Michael Mullen from "nonbattle" causes, his parents' opposition to the war, and their efforts to uncover the true circumstances of his death. [+]

Caputo, Philip. *A Rumor of War.* New York: Holt, Rinehart & Winston, 1977.

This is one of the major books of Vietnam War literature. Caputo was a young Marine infantry officer for sixteen months in Vietnam, beginning in 1965. He presents a grim, honest picture of the war. He recounts that the soldiers' enemies were boredom and climate as much as the Vietcong. Caputo provides an effective feeling for what fighting in Vietnam was really like. An excerpt appears in *The Wounded Generation: America after Vietnam.* [+]

Downs, Frederick. *Aftermath: A Soldier's Return from Vietnam.* New York: Norton, 1984.

In this narrative, Downs, who was severely wounded in Vietnam when he stepped on a land mine, tells the story of his recovery after many operations and how he rebuilt his life. [+]

————. *The Killing Zone: My Life in the Vietnam War.* New York: Norton, 1978.

The author tells the story of his life as an infantry lieutenant and leader of the first platoon of Delta Company, 3rd Brigade, in Duc Pho. Downs describes his efforts to keep his men safe, and his personal growth through the ordeal of combat. [+/–]

Edelman, Bernard, ed. *Dear America: Letters Home from Vietnam.* New York: Norton, 1985.

This is a collection of letters home from those serving and working in Vietnam during the war in all areas from soldiers to donut dollies. The last chapter, "Last Letters," is powerful and heartbreaking. This book was the basis for the outstanding made-for-cable-television film of the same title. Proceeds from this book helped finance the Vietnam Veterans Memorial in New York. This book is highly recommended for teenagers. [+]

Ehrhart, W. D. *Marking Time.* New York: Avon, 1986.

The author describes his experiences when he returns home from the war and enrolls as a student at Swarthmore College where he attempts to come to terms with his experiences and the campus antiwar protests.

————. *Vietnam Perkasie: A Combat Marine Memoir.* Jefferson, N.C.: McFarland, 1983.

Ehrhart recounts his Marine service in Vietnam, as well as his youth, basic training, and return home from the war.

Front Lines: *Soldiers' Writings from Vietnam.* Cambridge, Mass.: Indochina Curriculum Group, 1975.

A collection of personal narratives, letters, and excerpts from diaries of Vietnam veterans. This book is designed for use as a teaching tool for high school students.

Glasser, Ronald J. *365 Days.* New York: Braziller, 1971.

An important book in Vietnam War literature. It is well-written and contains elements of memoir, oral history, and fiction. Glasser was an Army doctor who relates his experiences in Zama Hospital in Japan. A number of the vignettes are excellent and have been anthologized. Selections are in *Touring Nam: The Vietnam War Reader* and *Words of War: An Anthology of Vietnam War Literature.* [–]

Goff, Stanley, and Robert Sanders, with Clark Smith. *Brothers: Black Soldiers in the Nam.* Novato, Calif.: Presidio Press, 1982.

The authors are two black Vietnam veterans who met in 1968 and became friends. They describe military training and focus on what it was like to be a black soldier in Vietnam. Two good selections have been anthologized in *Touring Nam: The Vietnam War Reader.* [–]

Goldman, Peter, and Tony Fuller. *Charlie Company.* New York: Morrow, 1983.

Newsweek reporters questioned the sixty-five infantrymen of Charlie Company about their experiences in Vietnam. The result is this history of the men of one combat company of 18–20-year-olds. The most interesting part is when the men talk of the silence they encountered when they came home.

Greene, Bob. *Homecoming: When the Soldiers Returned from Vietnam.* New York: G. P. Putnam's Sons, 1989.

This is a heartbreaking collection of letters by Vietnam veterans who wrote to author and syndicated columnist Bob Greene after he had asked his readers whether anyone had spat upon them when they were returning home from the war. It reports on the collision between the war in Asia and the war the vets faced on American soil. Very readable and certainly appropriate for most secondary students and perhaps capable upper-elementary students. [+]

Hayslip, Le Ly, with Jay Wurts. *When Heaven and Earth Changed Places.* New York: Doubleday, 1989.

The author, a Vietnamese woman who now lives in southern California, describes her experiences during the war. She vividly describes her life as a poor village girl who was forced to give her allegiance to the Communist army by night and to the South Vietnamese government by day. Danger and poverty forced her into the urban netherworld, where many Vietnamese learned to thrive in an atmosphere of black marketing and prostitution. Like some other Vietnamese women, she found escape by marrying an American. [–]

Herr, Michael. *Dispatches.* New York: Knopf, 1977.

This is considered by many to be one of the best Vietnam books. It describes what it was like to fight in the Vietnam War. The book has been described as "graphic, surrealistic, terrifying." No book does a better job of capturing the *feel* of Vietnam. Herr first went to Vietnam in 1967 as a correspondent for *Esquire.* Selections have been anthologized in various college readers and rhetorics, and an interesting excerpt is in *The Wounded Generation: America after Vietnam.* [_/+/–]

Klein, Joe. *Payback: Five Marines after Vietnam.* New York: Knopf, 1984.

Klein traced the lives of five Marines for fifteen years from the battles they shared in "Operation Cochise" in 1967 through their turbulent reentry into American society. This is the story of the difficulty of many veterans to readjust to life in peacetime, as well as the confused attitudes of those who received them home. [+]

Kovic, Ron. *Born on the Fourth of July.* New York: McGraw-Hill, 1976.

Kovic's book is considered one of the classics in Vietnam War literature. He describes his idealistic enlistment in the Marines, his service in Vietnam, his painful return home in a wheelchair, and his treatment at the hands of the Veterans Administration. He also tells of his involvement in the antiwar movement, attending the Republican Convention, and disrupting Nixon's acceptance speech. Oliver Stone's excellent movie version makes this an even better book to use in the classroom. [+/–]

Lowry, Timothy S. *And Brave Men, Too.* New York: Crown, 1985.

The author served two tours in Vietnam and is now a journalist who traveled across the U.S. interviewing recipients of the Congressional Medal of Honor. He includes the stories of fourteen soldiers told in chronological order which give an overview of the war and its costs in human terms.

McConnell, Malcolm. *Into the Mouth of the Cat: The Story of Lance Sijan, Hero of Vietnam.* New York: Norton, 1985.

This is an inspiring story of a pilot who was shot down over Laos. He was severely crippled, but evaded capture for 146 days. Once captured, he was put in the Bamboo Prison Camp. He then escaped but was recaptured, tortured, and died in Hanoi of untreated wounds. His example was an inspiration to other American prisoners to resist torture.

McCloud, Bill. *What Should We Tell Our Children about Vietnam?* Norman: University of Oklahoma Press, 1989.

The author, a Vietnam veteran and junior high school social studies teacher, wondered what to tell his students about Vietnam. He wrote to the people who directed, fought, protested, and reported the war. These 128 letters form a remarkable cross-section of public opinion from statesmen, veterans, protestors, writers, and others. Some of the contributing writers and filmmakers include Allen Ginsberg, Larry Heinemann, John Hersey, Ken Kesey, Tim O'Brien, Oliver Stone, Kurt Vonnegut, and many others. Appropriate for grades 6–college. [+]

Mailer, Norman. *The Armies of the Night: History as a Novel, The Novel as History.* New York: New American Library, 1968.

Mailer chronicles his adventures over the four days of the October 1967 anti-Vietnam demonstration in Washington, D.C., a history of the march on the Pentagon. The author captures the uncertainties, ambiguities, and hypocrisies of the period. [+]

Marshall, Kathryn. *In the Combat Zone: An Oral History of American Women in Vietnam, 1966–1975.* Boston: Little, Brown, 1987.

The author interviewed twenty women who tell about their experiences in the war. They relate their many motives for going to Vietnam, their experiences, and the impact the war had on their lives. The author interviewed army nurses, donut dollies, and civilians.

Mason, Robert. *Chickenhawk.* New York: Viking Press, 1983.

Mason was an assault helicopter pilot who flew over 1,000 combat missions during his tour of duty. His memoir is a vivid account of the life of these pilots. He discusses the frustration of taking the same patch of jungle over and over again, as well as the psychological effects of the war. He also discusses the shock of a hostile welcome home. [–]

Norton, Bruce H. *Force Recon Diary, 1969.* New York: Ivy Books, 1991.

A fascinating account of survival and death in one of the most highly skilled, elite units in Vietnam.

O'Brien, Tim. *If I Die in a Combat Zone.* New York: Delacorte, 1973.

This work is considered one of the best books to come out of the war. It is the story of one soldier's journey from safe, middle-class America to the center of the horror of the Vietnam War. O'Brien emphasizes the fear and the moral dilemmas. This work has been described as "new journalism," and in 1973 it was named ALA Best Book for Young Adults. A number of excerpts have been anthologized. One of the best, "Centurion," appears in *How We Live*, which is part of the Scholastic American Literature Program, Michael Spring, ed., 1977. A number of excerpts are in *Touring Nam: The Vietnam War Reader.* [+]

Palmer, Laura. *Shrapnel in the Heart: Letters and Remembrances from the Vietnam Veterans Memorial.* New York: Random House, 1987.

This is a collection of written mementos left at the Vietnam Veterans Memorial in Washington, D.C. Palmer is a reporter who was assigned to Vietnam and covered the fall of Saigon. She picked 100 letters left at the wall and traced the letter writers across the country to hear their stories. Wittman (1989) says that it is "a powerful but sad book to read."

Santoli, Al. *Everything We Had: An Oral History of the Vietnam War by Thirty-three American Soldiers Who Fought It.* New York: Random House, 1981.

This is an interesting and effective oral history of thirty-three veterans that takes the reader from 1962 through the fall of Saigon. The collection emphasizes their experiences in Vietnam. [+/–]

———. *To Bear Any Burden: The Vietnam War and Its Aftermath in the Words of Americans and Southeast Asians.* New York: Dutton, 1985.

This oral history explores the human side of war in a series of forty-eight personal accounts by Vietnamese and Americans before, during, and after the war. Those who speak, attempt to discover the meaning of the war.

Sheehan, Neil. *A Bright Shining Lie: John Paul Vann and America in Vietnam.* New York: Random House, 1988.

Ten years in preparation, Sheehan's book tells the story of John Vann, a flawed hero who became the "Lawrence of Arabia" of Vietnam, eventually dying in a helicopter crash in 1972. The book won the 1988 Pulitzer Prize and provides good historical background on the war.

Terry, Wallace. *Bloods: An Oral History of the Vietnam War by Black Veterans.* New York: Random House, 1984.

Terry presents the war experiences of twenty black soldiers. He argues that black soldiers made up a large percentage of those who fought in Vietnam. Blacks accounted for 23 percent of all American fatalities. [+/–]

Troung Nhu Tang, with David Chanoff and Doan Van Toai. *A Vietcong Memoir.* New York: Harcourt Brace Jovanovich, 1985.

Troung Nhu Tang was the Minister of Justice for the Vietcong Provisional Government and founder of the National Liberation Front. He tells the political story from the Vietcong point of view. He notes that the new Vietnam is as unjust as the old. He now lives in exile.

Van Devanter, Lynda, with Christopher Morgan. *Home before Morning: The Story of an Army Nurse in Vietnam.* New York: Beaufort Books, 1983.

> The author tells of her experiences during her tour of duty; her change from an idealist who once viewed the war as a chance to save a country from communist control; the problems she had when she returned home, including being treated as "a murderer rather than a healer"; and her experiences with posttraumatic stress disorder. This is a powerful narrative. [+/–]

Walker, Keith. *A Piece of My Heart: The Stories of 26 American Women Who Served in Vietnam.* Novato, Calif.: Presidio Press, 1985.

> Walker has put together twenty-six stories of a representative sample of the 15,000 women who served in Vietnam—nurses, WACS, USO and Red Cross workers, entertainers, and civilian volunteers. This is an interesting study of the women who served in Vietnam. [+]

Willenson, Kim. *The Bad War: An Oral History of the Vietnam War.* New York: New American Library, 1987.

> The author describes how the United States got involved in Vietnam, what we did there, what it did to us, why and how we got out, and what it has meant to both the U.S. and Vietnam since. This book is excellent and useful because the voices that discuss these issues represent people on both sides, the ordinary and the famous.

Woolf, Cecil, and John Bagguley, eds. *Authors Take Sides on Vietnam.* New York: Simon and Schuster, 1967.

> The editors asked hundreds of distinguished writers to briefly answer two questions: "Are you for or against the intervention of the United States in Vietnam?" And, "How, in your opinion, should the conflict in Vietnam be resolved?" The 168 published answers provide a fascinating collection of diverse opinions on the war from writers such as James Baldwin, Nathaniel Benchley, Lawrence Ferlinghetti, Denise Levertov, Arthur Miller, Susan Sontag, and Richard Wilbur. [+]

Zumwalt, Elmo, III, and Elmo R. Zumwalt, Jr. *My Father, My Son.* New York: Macmillan, 1986.

> Elmo R. Zumwalt III volunteered for Vietnam rather than make use of his position as the son of Admiral Zumwalt to avoid the military. He served with distinction, and after returning home, he got married and had children. Lieutenant Zumwalt had been exposed to Agent Orange, which was sprayed along the rivers he and his crew patrolled. In 1983, he developed cancer,

and his son was born with a rare birth defect. Ironically, it was his father who had given the order to spray the defoliant. The Zumwalts recount their story and vividly describe their attempt to cope with the tragedy and its attendant guilt.

Novels

Amos, James. *The Memorial: A Novel of Vietnam.* New York: Avon Books, 1989.

> A Vietnam veteran visits the black granite memorial in Washington, D.C. The visit reawakens the war for former Marine Lieutenant Jack Adams and forces him to relive his experiences.

Anderson, Kent. *Sympathy for the Devil.* Garden City, N.Y.: Doubleday, 1987.

> This is an effective novel in which the main character, Hanson, comes to Vietnam as a naive, liberal, college-educated young man. After a series of atrocities and deaths, the horror of battle, and the despair of the war, Hanson becomes a hardened soldier.

Baber, Asa. *The Land of a Million Elephants.* New York: Morrow, 1970.

> Told in the manner of an ancient folktale, this novel tells the story of the land of Chanda, which resists the attempts of outsiders to bring a neighboring war to its land. This antiwar story contrasts the horrors of Vietnam and Laos with echoes of a better time and place that are now only a fantasy.

Bennett, Jack. *The Voyage of the Lucky Dragon.* Englewood Cliffs, N.J.: Prentice-Hall, 1982.

> After the fall of Saigon, a Vietnamese family flees the Communist reeducation camps in a fishing boat bound for Australia. Written for grades 7–9.

Bograd, Larry. *Travelers.* New York: Lippincott, 1986.

> A boy is haunted by the image of the father he never knew, who died in Vietnam. He tries to find out more about him. Written for high school students.

Boyd, Candy Dawson. *Charlie Pippin.* New York: Macmillan, 1987.

> The father of eleven-year-old Charlie returns home from Vietnam a bitter, rigid man. Charlie tries to understand her father by studying about the Vietnam War. She discovers that her father is a decorated war hero. The novel examines how too many blacks had to fight the war. Written for grades 5–7.
> [+]

Butler, Robert Olen. *The Alleys of Eden.* New York: Horizon Press, 1981.

> After marrying his college sweetheart, Cliff Wilkes is drafted and sent to Vietnam. He serves well, until his marriage comes to an end, and he is involved in a Vietcong prisoner's death. He deserts and lives with a Vietnamese bar girl. After the fall of Saigon, Cliff returns home to Illinois with his Vietnamese girlfriend where neither of them is able to fit in, and he is still a fugitive.

Caputo, Philip. *Indian Country.* New York: Bantam, 1987.

> This is a powerful novel about a Vietnam veteran who, several years after coming home, has not resolved painful wartime experiences, especially the death of a boyhood friend. The anger and passion that he can no longer suppress threaten to destroy all he has grown to love.

Coonts, Stephen. *Flight of the Intruder.* Annapolis, Md.: Naval Institute Press, 1986.

> Coonts, an ex-Navy flier, tells the story of Jake Grafton, a Navy pilot who flies air raids over North Vietnam from the deck of an aircraft carrier. Jake worries about the deaths he causes but does not see from his plane. When his best friend is killed, he sets out to bomb the Communist Party headquarters in Hanoi.

Crosby, Alexander. *One Day for Peace.* Boston: Little, Brown, 1971.

> Jane Simon is a junior high school student who is very upset over the death of her friend, the milkman, in Vietnam. She writes a letter to the president asking him to tell her why the U.S. is fighting, and organizes a committee in her town to plan a peace parade. Written for grades 6–10.

Currey, Richard. *Fatal Light.* New York: Dutton/Seymour Lawrence, 1988.

> Currey tells the story of a combat medic in Vietnam. The young medic in this rite of passage book comes of age as he sees sickness, poverty, and the horrible deaths of soldiers and civilians. Juxtaposed with the ugliness of war are the fond memories of his home, his family, and his girlfriend which the medic shares with the reader.

Del Vecchio, John M. *The 13th Valley.* New York: Bantam, 1982.

> This is one of the best of the Vietnam War novels; it tells the story of three men involved in a major combat mission in the Khe Ta Laou Valley in 1970. The book contains realistic portrayals of the men and their fears before and in battle. The author also describes the companionship the men find in each other, and their actions in the final jungle battle. [_/+/–]

Dodge, Ed. *Dau: A Novel of Vietnam*. New York: Macmillan, 1984.

> This is a very well-written and powerful novel. The hero, Morgan Preston, goes to Vietnam in 1965 and is assigned to a unit that transports supplies, the wounded, and the dead by helicopter. He tells his story and that of the men he knows. When Morgan returns home, he is physically and mentally wounded himself. He spends time in a mental institution, trying to deal with his experiences. [_/+/–]

Durden, Charles. *No Bugles, No Drums*. New York: Viking Press, 1976.

> This is an interesting story of Jamie Hawkins, a southern soldier who feels he has somehow stumbled into a surreal movie in Vietnam. He struggles against the army and everything around him, trying to hold on to his sanity. The story is told in the first person, and Jamie recounts the death of his best friend and the traitorous activities of another soldier whom he later kills. [_/–]

Eastlake, William. *The Bamboo Bed*. New York: Simon & Schuster, 1969.

> This novel is considered by many to be the *Catch-22* of this war. The main characters are Captain Knightbridge and his aide, Lt. Janine Bliss, who involve themselves in nonmilitary matters in the helicopter, The Bamboo Bed, above the battles, and Captain Clancy, an old-fashioned soldier, who fights the war on the ground. The novel has been called "surreal, blackly humorous, and heavily symbolic." [_/–]

Ford, Daniel. *Incident at Muc Wa*. Garden City, N.Y.: Doubleday, 1967.

> A well-written novel which features Cpl. Stephen Courcey, a demolitions expert working in the highlands with a group of commanding officers who are nothing less than fools. The remote camp at Muc Wa is held through several attacks but finally lost, and the main character is killed. This book was reissued in 1979 by Jove under the title *Go Tell the Spartans*, the same title as the film based on the book, which is available on videotape.

Fuller, Jack. *Fragments*. New York: Morrow, 1984.

> This is one of the major Vietnam novels. It is a vivid account of the wartime experience and a friendship between two men. Morgan and Newmann volunteer for a special missions team. The two soldiers symbolize different points of view about how to survive. Newmann believes in free will and is an instinctive fighter. He feels he must take charge. On the other hand, Morgan is a more cautious person, who believes in fate and in letting others decide what is best. In the course of the story, both are wounded, and Newmann kills a Vietnamese family. [+/–]

Gilson, Jamie. *Hello, My Name Is Scrambled Eggs.* New York: Lothrop, 1985.

> Tuan Nguyen is a Vietnamese refugee who arrives in the U.S. to live with the Trumble family in a small town in Illinois. Their son, Harvey, is a seventh grader who tries to mold him into an "American kid." Written for grades 4–7.

Glasser, Ronald. *Another War, Another Peace.* New York: Summit, 1985.

> This is a well-written novel by the author of *365 Days*. It tells the story of the growing friendship between two men: David, a young doctor sent to Vietnam, and his driver, Tom. [+]

Graham, Gail. *Cross-Fire: A Vietnam Novel.* New York: Pantheon, 1972.

> This is the story of an American soldier who becomes separated from his unit. He meets four Vietnamese children, the only survivors of a raid on their village. Although there is mutual hate and suspicion, they band together for safety and try to get to civilization. All five are eventually killed by Americans. Written for grades 7–12.

Greene, Graham. *The Quiet American.* New York: Viking Press, 1955.

> This book has been called "one of the most influential and prophetic novels of Vietnam War literature." It describes American involvement in Vietnam before it actually happened. This is the story of a jaded British war correspondent in Saigon whose uninvolved life is upset by a young American government agent who falls in love with the correspondent's Vietnamese mistress. The American is full of good intentions, but his naivete leads to trouble. [+]

Groom, Winston. *Better Times Than These.* New York: Summit Books, 1978.

> This important novel tells the story of Bravo Company in Vietnam in 1966. The men of the company endure a long sea voyage and then a long jungle trek before engaging in a battle that kills many of them. The author describes the interactions of the men, their relationships with people back home, the dangers of the jungle, and the loss of friends in an engrossing manner that reveals the reality of the daily life of a soldier in Vietnam.

Hahn, Mary Downing. *December Stillness.* New York: Clarion, 1989.

> Thirteen-year-old Kelly McAlister gains an enriched view of life beyond the routine of school when she attempts to befriend Mr. Weems, a disturbed, homeless Vietnam War veteran. In the process of helping him, Kelly grows emotionally and acquires social awareness and responsibility. Appropriate for grades 5–12. [+]

Halberstam, David. *One Very Hot Day.* New York: Warner, 1984.

> One of the major novels, this one tells the story of what should have been an easy assault on a Vietcong rest camp across the Ap Thamh Thoi canal. However, something goes terribly wrong and the Americans fall into a trap. The story is told from the point of view of two Americans who led the raid and of the Vietnamese lieutenant who countered it. The action takes place on one day.

Hasford, Gustav. *The Short-Timers.* New York: Harper and Row, 1979.

> Marine William "Joker" Doolittle is sent to Vietnam as a combat reporter. Toward the end of his tour, his negative attitude earns him a place in a military action in Hue during the Tet Offensive. He becomes a leader. The surreal quality so evident in many Vietnam novels is an important characteristic of this major work. The film *Full Metal Jacket* was based on this novel. [_/+/–]

Heckler, Jonellen. *Safekeeping.* New York: Putnam, 1983.

> Judy Greer is the wife of a POW held by the North Vietnamese. She has never received a letter from him since his capture several years before. Her involvement in antiwar activities has alienated her from her twelve-year-old son, Kevin. Kevin's football coach, Major Joseph Campbell, comes into their lives and brings what each needs, but his arrival forces a difficult choice.

Heinemann, Larry. *Close Quarters.* New York: Farrar, Straus & Giroux, 1974.

> This classic novel of the war follows the coming of age of Philip Dosier and his fellow soldiers in Vietnam, where they learn that war is nothing like a John Wayne movie. Dosier returns home stunned by his experiences and deadened to emotions. [+/–]

———. *Paco's Story.* New York: Farrar, Straus & Giroux, 1986.

> The National Book Award winner for 1988, this is the story of the sole survivor of a devastating Vietcong attack who returns to civilian life as a dishwasher in a small-town cafe. His tale of horror is rendered in graphic detail by a hip-talking narrator, a dead soldier who speaks to the reader from beyond the grave. [+/–]

Hoover, Paul. *Saigon, Illinois.* New York: Vintage, 1988.

> The main character, Jim Holder, is granted conscientious objector status and must travel to Chicago from Indiana to do his alternative service in a hospital. The deaths he witnesses at the hospital and ones in Vietnam that he sees on the television each night keep the war very close to him.

Huggett, William Turner. *Body Count.* New York: Putnam, 1973.

> In this well-received novel, Lt. Chris Hawkins is the commander of a Marine platoon. The reader follows him through combat at Khe Sanh, R&R in Tokyo, and back to Vietnam for a terrible battle in which a hill is taken and then given up the very next day. This is a well-written novel with effective action scenes. [+/–]

Mason, Bobbie Ann. *In Country.* South Yarmouth, Mass: Curley, 1985.

> An effective and powerful novel, *In Country* tells the story of Samantha Hughes, a recent high school graduate who wants some answers about the Vietnam War. Her father was killed in the war. Her mother can't really tell her anything about her father since they were married only a month before his death. Her uncle, Emmett, with whom she lives, could be suffering ill effects from Agent Orange exposure in Vietnam, and she is attracted to another Vietnam vet who is emotionally scarred by the war. While not specifically written for adolescents, this book is highly recommended for teenagers. [+]

Miller, Kenn. *Tiger, the Lurp Dog.* Boston: Little, Brown, 1983.

> A well-written and exciting story that focuses on American paratroopers of a Long-Range Reconnaissance Patrol (LRRP) in Vietnam. The men feel pride in their unit, whose mascot is a flea-bitten dog called Tiger. When part of the team disappears on a mission, the men plan and carry out a mission to find the missing team members.

Myers, Walter Dean. *Fallen Angels.* New York: Scholastic Books, 1988.

> A very powerful Vietnam War novel written for teenagers, *Fallen Angels* tells the story of Richie Perry, 17, who enlists to fight in Vietnam as a way out of a dead-end life in Harlem. He experiences all of the horrors of war as well as the racial conflict that existed among American troops. Richie questions his religious faith and his moral values. This book is highly recommended for teenagers. [+]

O'Brien, Tim. *Going after Cacciato.* New York: Delacorte, 1978.

> This 1979 National Book Award winner is an account of a soldier's flight from battle that alternates between fantasy and reality. Paul Berlin, shocked by the horror and hopelessness of the war, walks away from his unit into the jungle, hoping to make his way to Paris. He is pursued by a group of soldiers. [_/+]

———. *The Things They Carried.* New York: Houghton Mifflin, 1990.

> An unusual novel in which war stories are told by various characters and narrators who sometimes retell in different

ways stories already told. Narrators dispute the accuracy of what they themselves are saying. Occasionally a narrator will come to the end of a harrowing tale and then insist that the protagonist did not do the terrible or heroic things he has just recited, but that he himself did them. [_/+/–]

Paterson, Katherine. *Park's Quest.* New York: Dutton, 1988.

The author describes the effects of the war on the children of those who served. The main character, Park, comes to his grandfather's farm in Virginia to learn more about his father, who died in Vietnam, and his father's family. He meets a Vietnamese-American girl named Thanh, who may be his half-sister. Written for young readers. [+]

Proffitt, Nicholas. *The Embassy House.* New York: Bantam, 1986.

In this novel, Operation Phoenix, which finds and eliminates Vietcong from local villages, is described. Led by Capt. Jack Gulliver, the operation gains unwanted public attention when an innocent man is killed and a cover-up of its activities is ordered. Those closest to Gulliver are exposed, and he is forced to come to terms with the conflict between his military assignment and his own values.

———. *Gardens of Stone.* New York: Carroll & Graf, 1983.

An interesting novel that describes the friendship of two men who are assigned to the Honor Guard at Arlington National Cemetery in 1966. Also involved in their story is a young soldier who will be sent to Vietnam and killed. This is a story of friendship, love, duty, and the waste of war.

Riggin, Rob. *Free Fire Zone.* New York: Norton, 1984.

The main character, Jon O'Neill, was a medic in Vietnam. He remembers and relates his tour of duty in flashback. The author describes the internal conflicts between the men and the effect of the war on their spirits. [_/+/–]

Roth, Robert. *Sand in the Wind.* Boston: Little, Brown, 1973.

One of the major novels, *Sand in the Wind* contains well-developed characters and effective battle scenes. It is the story of two soldiers, an officer and an enlisted man, in Vietnam around the time of Tet. In addition, the author shows the brutality of basic training and atrocities committed by both American and South Vietnamese soldiers. [–]

Rubin, Jonathan. *The Barking Deer.* New York: George Braziller, 1974.

Based on a Vietnamese fable in which a tiger and an eagle fight to protect the very fragile barking deer, who is destroyed as a result, this novel depicts the relationship between Special

Forces and Montagnard tribesmen in Vietnam early in the war. Ultimately, this well-written novel shows the Americans' inability to understand the Vietnamese.

Rylant, Cynthia. *A Blue-Eyed Daisy.* New York: Bradbury, 1985.

In this novel for young readers, eleven-year-old Ellie Farley's uncle Joe goes off to war. She is confused about wars and men killing one another and even more confused by her uncle's silence upon his return. [+]

Schaeffer, Susan Fromberg. *Buffalo Afternoon.* New York: Knopf, 1989.

The son of Italian immigrants, Pete Bravado is an unusually sensitive boy growing up in Brooklyn. Problems with his father and brushes with the law lead him to enlist in the Army, which sends him to Vietnam. He learns truths about himself, about life, and about death. These experiences handicap him when he returns home and tries to build a life for himself because he is "out of sync" with how others around him view life. This is a well-written novel. [_/+/–]

Sloan, James Park. *War Games.* Boston: Houghton Mifflin, 1971.

The narrator of this effective and well-written novel is a young soldier who wants to write the great novel of the Vietnam War. He gets transferred to Vietnam, but what he finds is a world full of corruption and petty bureaucracy, as well as the death and dying he sees on the combat mission he accompanies. [-]

Stone, Robert. *Dog Soldiers.* Boston: Houghton Mifflin, 1974.

Winner of the National Book Award, *Dog Soldiers* is one of the major novels of the war. The hero is John Converse, a newspaperman who collapsed in terror during a bombing in Cambodia. He subsequently acquires heroin and becomes involved in drug smuggling. He and his wife become addicted as well. Stone does a particularly effective job of describing the effect of war on noncombatants both in Vietnam and at home. [-]

Surat, Michelle Maria. *Angel Child, Dragon Child.* Milwaukee: Raintree, 1983.

A children's picture book that tells the story of a Vietnamese refugee child trying to adjust to an American school. Pictures by Vo-Dinh Mai. Grades K–3.

Tran, Khan Tuyet. *The Little Weaver of Thai-Yen Village.* San Francisco: Children's Book Press, 1977.

Written in English and Vietnamese, this book tells the story of Hien, a Vietnamese girl who is brought to the U.S. for medical treatment after the loss of her family. She describes her wartime experiences, which are intended to help American children understand the experiences of refugee children. Translated by N. H. Jenkins, with illustrations by Nancy Hom, this book, which was revised in 1986, was written for children in grades 3-6.

Wartski, Maureen Crane. *A Boat to Nowhere*. Philadelphia: Westminster, 1980.

Villagers protest Thay Van Chi's protection of a wandering orphan. They seem to be right when the boy appears to side with the Vietcong when they arrive. What the villagers do not realize is that the boy is acting so that he will have an opportunity to save them. The villagers become boat people and must endure terrible hardships and dangers. This novel is written for elementary and junior high school students, as well as less able high school readers. [+]

Webb, James. *Fields of Fire*. Englewood Cliffs, N.J.: Prentice-Hall, 1978.

In this major novel of the Vietnam War, a Marine unit fights the Vietcong, endures unbelievable living conditions, confronts the dangers of the "bush," and faces death and injury. Webb explores the reasons each man became a Marine, as the reader follows him through combat. The novel also examines the difficulties veterans face when they return home. [+/–]

Wolitzer, Meg. *Caribou*. New York: Bantam, 1986.

Becca Silverman, a twelve-year-old, is troubled by the Vietnam War; in fact, by the idea of war in general. Her brother escapes to Canada to avoid the draft. She decides to paint a vivid antiwar picture as her entry in the school's art contest, whose theme is patriotism. Written for grades 4-7. [+]

Wolkoff, Judie. *Where the Elf King Sings*. Scarsdale, N.Y.: Bradbury, 1980.

Twelve-year-old Marcie struggles to deal with her alcoholic father, a Vietnam veteran who is not able to come to terms with the war. His traumatic experiences in the war have cast a shadow over the whole family for the six years he has been home. This book is written for grades 6-9. [+]

Wright, Stephen. *Meditations in Green*. New York: Scribner's, 1983.

James Griffin, who will later refer to his time in Vietnam as "the lost years," was never an optimistic soldier in the war. His experiences in Vietnam turned him into a drug addict and made his readjustment after his return home painful. This is one of the major Vietnam War novels. [_/+/–]

Drama

Cole, Tom. *Medal of Honor Rag.* New York: French, 1977. Also in
  Coming to Terms: American Plays and the Vietnam War.

> In this one-act play, a psychiatrist, who is also a concentration
> camp survivor, does his best to help a black Vietnam War
> veteran suffering from the delayed stress caused by the war.
> [+/−]

Coming to Terms: American Plays and the Vietnam War. New York: Theatre
  Communications Group, 1985.

> A collection of seven plays about the Vietnam War. The plays
> reflect a wide range of emotions generated by the war. The
> plays included are David Rabe's *Streamers,* Terrence McNally's
> *Boticelli,* Amlin Gray's *How I Got That Story,* Tom Cole's *Medal of
> Honor Rag,* Michael Weller's *Moonchildren,* Emily Mann's *Still
> Life,* and Stephen Metcalfe's *Strange Snow.* [+/−]

Gray, Amlin. *How I Got That Story.* New York: Dramatists Play Service,
  1981. Also in *Coming to Terms: American Plays and the Vietnam War.*

> A two-act play that involves a journalist who is sent to a
> country very much like Vietnam during the war. As he sends
> back the reports of the war, he becomes more and more
> disillusioned.

Kopit, Arthur. *Indians.* New York: Hill & Wang, 1969.

> This is a political allegory about Vietnam disguised as the story
> of Buffalo Bill and Sitting Bull.

Kubrick, Stanley, Michael Herr, and Gustav Hasford. *Full Metal Jacket.*
  New York: Knopf, 1987.

> This is the screenplay from the movie that was based on
> Hasford's *The Short-Timers.* [+/−]

Metcalfe, Stephen. *Strange Snow.* New York: Theatre Communications
  Group, 1982. Also in *Coming to Terms: American Plays and the
  Vietnam War.*

> The play focuses on two Vietnam buddies, Dave and Megs.
> Megs comes to Dave's home to take him fishing on opening
> day. Dave holds Megs responsible for the death of their friend,
> Bobby, in Vietnam since Bobby had died saving Megs, who
> was wounded. It turns out that Dave hadn't wanted Bobby to
> go back for Megs. Metcalfe wrote the screenplay for the film
> version of this play entitled *Jacknife.*

Rabe, David. *The Basic Training of Pavlo Hummel* and *Sticks and Bones.*
  New York: Viking Press, 1973.

Unquestionably, these are two of the major Vietnam plays. *The Basic Training of Pavlo Hummel* tells the story of the basic training, army life, and death of a U.S. soldier in Vietnam. The story is told either in flashback or remembered in the last moments of his life. [+] In *Sticks and Bones,* David is a blind Vietnam veteran. He is goaded into suicide by his mother and father, Ozzie and Harriet, and his brother Ricky.

———. *Streamers.* New York: Knopf, 1975.

Set in an army barracks early in the war, *Streamers* tells the story of six very different soldiers awaiting orders to Vietnam. While waiting for their orders, they fight over various things. [–]

Ribman, Ronald. *The Burial of Esposito.* In *Best Short Plays, 1971.* Edited by Stanley Richards. Radnor, Pa.: Chilton, 1971, 157–70.

A father must confront the war when his son is killed in Vietnam.

———. *The Final War of Ollie Winter.* In "CBS Playhouse Presents: 'The Final War of Ollie Winter.'" New York: CBS Television Network, 1967.

This is a play written for television. The hero is a black soldier who tries to remain human—and humane—within the horror of the Vietnam War. The play may also be found in *Great Television Plays,* edited by William I. Kaufman (New York: Dell, 1969), 259–301. A shorter version is in Robert C. Pooley et al, *Perspectives.* Galaxy Series. Glenview, Ill.: Scott, Foresman, 1969, 363–401. This play is appropriate for grades 7–12. [+]

Stone, Oliver, and Richard Boyle. *Platoon.* In *Oliver Stone's "Platoon" and "Salvador": The Original Screenplays.* New York: Vintage, 1985.

This is the screenplay from the movie *Platoon.* [–]

Wilson, Lanford. *The 5th of July.* New York: Dramatists Play Service, 1982.

Over the 4th of July holiday, a legless Vietnam veteran, Ken Talley, hosts a party for ex-Berkeley radicals from the 1960s. All have been scarred in some way by their experiences during the Vietnam War.

Poetry

Balaban, John. *After Our War.* Pittsburgh: University of Pittsburgh, 1974.

A poetic picture of the effects of the Vietnam War on the Vietnamese people and their culture by a major poet in

Vietnam War literature. Not all of the poems in the collection deal with Vietnam.

———. *Blue Mountain.* Greensboro, N.C.: Unicorn Press, 1979.

While most of the poems in this collection focus on Balaban's experiences hitchhiking across the country, the second part includes seven Vietnam poems.

———. *Vietnam Poems.* Oxford: Carcanet Press, 1970.

Most of these poems present images of the lives of the Vietnamese peasants.

Barry, Jan, and W. D. Ehrhart, eds. *Demilitarized Zones.* Perkasie, Pa.: East River Anthology, 1976.

This is an important and powerful collection of 180 poems by 100 veterans.

Barth, Robert L. *Forced Marching to the Styx: Vietnam War Poems.* Van Nuys, Calif.: Perivale Press, 1983.

A Vietnam veteran, Barth begins this collection of twenty-one poems with a quote from Graham Greene's *It's a Battlefield* that expresses the theme of the collection: "One did not question during the war why one fought; one waited till the war was over for that."

———. *A Soldier's Time: Vietnam War Poems.* Santa Barbara, Calif.: John Daniel, 1988.

An excellent collection of forty-five of the author's poems. He traces the history of Vietnam's wars from Dien Bien Phu through American involvement.

Casey, Michael. *Obscenities.* New Haven, Conn.: Yale University Press, 1972.

This is thought to be one of the most effective poetry collections to come out of the war. The author served as a military policeman on Vietnamese Highway One—the setting for most of the poems.

Ehrhart, W. D. *The Awkward Silence.* Stafford, Va.: Northwoods Press, 1980.

This is the author's poetic description of how his tour of duty in Vietnam changed him and made him redefine his concept of patriotism.

———. *To Those Who Have Gone Home Tired: New and Selected Poems.* New York: Thunder's Mouth, 1984.

Ehrhart describes these twenty-seven poems as poems of love and friendship after the madness of war. Some of the poems are from other collections of his work.

Ehrhart, W. D., ed. *Carrying the Darkness: American Indochina: The Poetry of the Vietnam War.* New York: Avon, 1985.

This collection includes the work of seventy-four poets—from soldiers to civilians, men and women, Asians and Americans—representative of the generation that was changed forever by the war. An excellent collection. [+]

Floyd, Bryan Alec. *The Long War Dead: An Epiphany 1st Platoon, U.S.M.C.* New York: Avon, 1976.

The author was a Marine in 1967 and '68. He describes a poetic platoon. Each of the forty-seven poems bears the name of a man. The poem is his story—or his epitaph. An excellent collection. [+]

Mason, Steve. *Johnny's Song.* New York: Bantam, 1986.

The author, a Vietnam veteran, presents eleven well-developed poems, in which he records his feelings about his experiences. The Vietnam Veterans Memorial, "The Wall," is the central image in the work. The collection begins with "The Wall Within," which was read at dedication ceremonies at the wall and read into the Congressional Record, and ends with "After the Reading of the Names."

Rottmann, Larry, Jan Barry, and Basil T. Paquet, eds. *Winning Hearts & Minds: War Poems by Vietnam Veterans.* New York: McGraw-Hill, 1972.

This excellent collection contains 106 poems by thirty-three poets. They are arranged in chronological order to describe a tour of duty in Vietnam. [+]

Weigl, Bruce. *The Monkey Wars.* Athens: University of Georgia Press, 1979.

A short collection of poems, eight of which are about the Vietnam War. They present graphic images of the horror of the war, especially for the civilians.

Short Stories

Abbot, Lee K. "The Viet Cong Love of Sgt. Donnie T. Bobo." In *Touring Nam*, 181–92.

The story of two friends who are tunnel rats, and the truths they discover about love and war. [+/–]

Aitken, James. "Lederer's Legacy." In *Free Fire Zone*, 80–96.

> The narrator of this story is a new guy in country who learns important truths about the war from a soldier named Lederer, whose tour of duty is nearly over. [_/+]

Anderson, Kent. "Sympathy for the Devil." In *Touring Nam*, 117–79.

> This novella focuses on the men of the special operations group, who had some very unusual and often secret combat missions. [_/–]

Baber, Asa. "The Ambush" (also known as "Ambush: Laos, 1960"). In *Touring Nam*, 94–101; *Tranquility Base and Other Stories.* Canton, N.Y.: Fiction International, 1979, 14–40; *Vietnam Anthology*, 165–71; and *Writing under Fire*, 130–35.

> The story of an American adviser in Laos in 1960. [+]

Bobrowsky, Igor. "The Courier." In *Free Fire Zone*, 98–107.

> The tale of a Marine courier who has seen too much war. [_/+/–]

Bunting, Josiah. "The Lionheads." In *Touring Nam*, 223–62.

> This is the story of what an ambitious general's decision means to those who have to execute the decision. [_]

Chatain, Robert. "On the Perimeter." In *Touring Nam*, 302–23; and in *Writing under Fire*, 209–26.

> The story of how a soldier sees the war from the bottom looking up. [_]

Davis, George. "Ben." In *Free Fire Zone*, 183–86.

> This tale focuses on a black pilot on R&R in Bangkok, Thailand, who has a drink with a black grunt in a bar. The pilot is forced to confront some truths about his role in the war.

Deighton, Len. "First Base." In *Eleven Declarations of War*. New York: Harcourt Brace Jovanovich, 1971, 98–105.

> A sort of science fiction-like tale of two young soldiers, one white and one black, who set off in a truck to deliver equipment to a base in the field. They become lost and end up at an abandoned American base where one of them dies. [_]

Ferry, James. "Dancing Ducks and Talking Anus." In *The Best American Short Stories, 1982*. John Gardner, ed., with Shannon Ravenel. Boston: Houghton Mifflin, 1982, 18–36.

> A complex story that deals with the violent behavior of a Vietnam veteran. [_/–]

Fowler, Karen Joy. "Letters from Home." In *In the Field of Fire*, 70–89.

A former antiwar activist writes a letter to a friend who was drafted and whom she never heard from again after he went into the military. In the letter, the narrator explores the impact of the war on those who came of age during the Vietnam War. [_/+]

Gerald, John Bart. "Walking Wounded." In *The Best American Short Stories, 1969*. Martha Foley and David Burnett, eds., Boston: Houghton Mifflin, 1969, 37–48; and *The Fact of Fiction: Social Relevance in the Short Story*, 112–21.

This is the story of a stateside hospital medic who works with wounded soldiers sent home from Vietnam. He does his best to avoid having to deal with the war, but eventually the horror of the war leaves him as wounded as those he cares for in the hospital. [+/–]

Grau, Shirley Ann. "Homecoming." In *Vietnam Anthology*, 56–65; and *The Wind Shifting West*. New York: Knopf, 1973, 41–54.

The story of how the death of a soldier in Vietnam brings the war home to a small-town young woman who once dated him in high school. [+]

Hannah, Barry. "Midnight and I'm Not Famous Yet." In *Airships*. New York: Knopf, 1978, 105–18.

The story of an airborne unit commander whose desire for a little reminder of home leads to the death of a hometown friend and a mistake in judgment in combat. Ultimately, the commander is relieved of his command, and he learns some important truths about the war. [+/–]

Heinemann, Larry. "The First Clean Fact." In *The Best American Short Stories, 1980*. Stanley Elkin and Shannon Ravenel, eds. Boston: Houghton Mifflin, 1980, 210–20; and *Vietnam Anthology*, 66–74.

A hip-talking dead soldier tells the story of how his whole company, except for one man, got killed. [_/+/–]

———. "God's Marvelous Plan." In *Harper's* 263 (August 1981): 54–60.

Heinemann's hip-talking ghost soldier tells the story of how the lone survivor of a company wiped out in an enemy attack survives and is rescued. [_/+/–]

———. "Good Morning to You, Lieutenant." In *Harper's* 260 (June 1980): 59–60, 64, 66–69; and in *Soldiers and Civilians*, 155–68.

The only survivor of the enemy attack on Fire Base Harriet returns home and tries to find peace in a small town. [_/+/–]

Huddle, David. "The Interrogation of the Prisoner Bung by Mr.
    Hawkins and Sergeant Tree." In *Free Fire Zone*, 59–67; and
    Vietnam Anthology, 37–44.

> This seemingly simple story about an American adviser, his
> translator, and the Vietcong suspect they interrogate is an
> allegory for much that was wrong with the Vietnam War. [_/+/
> –]

Karlin, Wayne. "Extract." In *Free Fire Zone*, 177–82.

> This is the tale of a Marine helicopter door gunner who has
> some doubts about firing on a village where the helicopter has
> been receiving enemy fire. [+/–]

———. "Medical Evacuation." In *Free Fire Zone*, 17–19.

> On a mission to pick up wounded Marines during Operation
> Hastings, Karlin's helicopter door gunner is forced to confront
> the realities of killing and death in war. [+/–]

———. "R&R." In *Free Fire Zone*, 136–43.

> While on R&R in Saigon, Karlin's gunner tries to escape the
> war in the nightclubs and bars on Tu Do Street. [–]

———. "Search and Destroy." In *Free Fire Zone*, 51–54.

> A group of Marines is bothered by rats in its tent and, as its
> own casualties increase, it begins to see the rats as the enemy.
> [–]

Kimpel, John M. "And Even Beautiful Hands Cry." In *Free Fire Zone*,
    69–79.

> The story of a Saigon warrior so far from the fighting that he
> thinks he can escape the war. When asked to help a woman's
> dying baby, the soldier must confront his role in the war. [–]

Little, Lloyd. "Out with the Lions." In *Free Fire Zone*, 41–50.

> A team of advisers operating with Nung mercenaries near the
> Cambodian border gets into a firefight with an enemy unit.
> The advisers appear to be in a bad situation until the Nungs
> discover that the enemy is another group of Nung mercenaries
> working for the Vietcong. [+]

McCammon, Robert R. "Nightcrawlers." In *Masques: All New Works of
    Horror and the Supernatural.* J. N. Williamson, ed. Baltimore:
    Maclay, 1984, 11–36.

> A terrifying tale of a Vietnam veteran suffering from survivor's
> guilt who shares his nightmares about Vietnam with patrons
> of an all-night diner. A good version of this story was made for
> the new "Twilight Zone" series. [+]

Mason, Bobbie Ann. "Big Bertha Stories." In *Soldiers and Civilians,* 202–16; and *Unwinding the Vietnam War: From War into Peace,* 121–33.

A seemingly happy Vietnam veteran suddenly begins having trouble with his job and family. In trying to cope, he creates a series of stories about the mythic Big Bertha. His marriage crumbling, the veteran finally seeks help. [_/+]

Mayer, Tom. "A Birth in the Delta." In *Touring Nam,* 339–57; and *Writing under Fire,* 43–57.

An infantry company on an operation in the Mekong Delta encounters a dying woman about to give birth. They try to save the baby but it is born dead. As a result, the men in the company confront some truths about the war, and they will never be the same again. [_/+/–]

Moore, Robin. "We Have Met the Enemy." In *Combat Pay.* New York: Manor Books, 1976, 181–86.

The story of two Marines who become separated from their platoon during a firefight and the shocking discovery they make after killing a shadowy figure who runs into a cave behind their position. [+]

———. "Welcome Home." In *Combat Pay.* New York: Manor Books, 1976, 220–27.

This story deals with the reality of what it was like for many veterans when they first arrived home from Vietnam. [+]

Mueller, Quentin. "Children Sleeping—Bombs Falling." In *Free Fire Zone,* 202–04.

At the end of his tour of duty a Marine encounters two children selling ice cream on a pier on a riverfront in Da Nang. The sounds of the war in the distance cause him to realize what the war has done to him and is doing to the children of Vietnam. [+]

Nguyen, Sang. "The Ivory Comb." In *Fragment from a Lost Diary and Other Stories: Women of Asia, Africa, and Latin America.* Naomi Katz and Nancy Milton, eds. New York: Pantheon Books, 229–43.

This is the story of a young Vietcong woman soldier and her uncle, who is finally able to deliver the ivory comb he has been carrying for her for years. The comb was given to him by the woman's father when he died in a bombing raid. [+]

Oates, Joyce Carol. "Out of Place." In *The Seduction and Other Stories.* Los Angeles: Black Sparrow Press, 1976, 154–64.

This is the story of a disabled Vietnam veteran who returns home to his family and community, only to discover that no one will accept him. [+]

O'Brien, Tim. "The Ghost Soldiers." In *Great Esquire Fiction: The Finest Stories*. Rust Hills, ed. New York: Viking Press, 1983, 494–515; and *Prize Stories, 1982: The O. Henry Awards*. William Abrahams, ed. Garden City, N.Y.: Doubleday, 1982, 206–28.

A soldier who is wounded in combat plots revenge on the new medic who nearly let him die. The revenge plan gets out of hand and the narrator must confront some truths about himself and war. [+]

———. "How to Tell a True War Story." *Esquire* 108 (October 1987): 208–15.

The narrator of this story tries to explain how to recognize a true war story and in the process tells some war stories that reveal what war is really all about. [_/+]

———. "Night March." In *Prize Stories, 1974: The O. Henry Awards*. William Abrahams, ed. Garden City, N.Y.: Doubleday, 1976, 211–19; and *Prize Stories of the Seventies: From the O. Henry Awards*. Garden City, N.Y.: Doubleday, 1981, 258–65.

This is the story of a new soldier in Vietnam who is trying to come to grips with his overpowering feelings of fear. [+]

———. "The Sweetheart of the Song Tra Bong." *Esquire* 112 (July 1989): 94–103.

The story of a seventeen-year-old American girl who comes to Vietnam to be with her childhood sweetheart, a medic at a remote outpost. Things go well for a brief period of time, but slowly she is caught up in the same forces that work on the soldiers. [+/–]

———. "The Things They Carried." In *The Best American Short Stories, 1987*. Ann Beattie, ed. Boston: Houghton Mifflin, 1987, 287–305; and in *Vietnam Anthology*, 79–94.

The narrator of this story explains what soldiers carried in the field in Vietnam. As the story develops, the narrator moves from the physical things to the emotional and psychological burdens. [+]

Pancake, Breece D'J. "The Honored Dead." In *Soldiers and Civilians*, 98–106; and *The Stories of Breece D'J Pancake*. Boston: Little, Brown, 1983, 115–25.

In this story a man tries to comfort his daughter, who is afraid of the dark, and in the process is reminded of his own fears as a young man. He remembers his best friend, who was killed in Vietnam, his own trick to avoid the draft, and the rift created between him and his father because he didn't want to go to Vietnam. [_]

Parker, Thomas. "Troop Withdrawal—The Initial Step." In *Prize Stories, 1971: The O. Henry Awards.* William Abrahams, ed. Garden City, N.Y.: Doubleday, 1971, 148–67; *Touring Nam,* 389–411; and *Writing under Fire,* 90–107.

This is the story of a clerk in a hospital unit who plots to kill, at least on paper, an officer whom he hates.

Paulsen, Gary. "The Second Kit Carson." In *The Best of the West.* Joe R. Landsdale, ed. Garden City, N.Y.: Doubleday, 1986, 23–36.

A traumatized and alcoholic Vietnam veteran is called upon to help a woman giving birth. The experience could enable him to get over his inability to deal with Vietnam. [+/–]

Perea, Robert L. "Small Arms Fire." In *Cuentos Chicanos: A Short Story Anthology.* Rudolfo A. Anaya and Antonio Marques, eds. Albuquerque: University of New Mexico Press, 1981, 358–65.

Two soldiers at a remote outpost encounter an officer who is so intent on getting a medal that he refuses to help a group of wounded South Vietnamese soldiers. [+]

Pitts, Oran R. "Temporary Duty." In *Free Fire Zone,* 126–34.

This is the story of a medic in a rear area aid station who is temporarily assigned to a hospital company near the front because of his negative attitude. At the end of his temporary duty his attitude has not changed, but he will never be the same again. [+/–]

Porsche, Don. "Evenings in Europe and Asia." In *Touring Nam,* 20–29; and *Writing under Fire,* 35–42.

A young soldier in Vietnam who went to college to avoid the draft remembers a conversation he had with a young German man who warned him about what would happen to him.

Rascoe, Judith. "Soldier, Soldier." In *Yours, and Mine: Novella and Stories.* Boston: Little, Brown, 1973, 164–79.

This is the story of an antiwar activist who, despite her hatred of the war, is attracted to a Vietnam veteran. [_/–]

Robinson, Kim Stanley. "The Memorial." In *In the Field of Fire,* 19–23.

The narrator of this story visits the Vietnam Veterans Memorial in Washington, D.C., and tries to understand what it means to her and to the nation. [+]

Rossman, Michael. "The Day We Named Our Child We Had Fish for Dinner." In *New American Review,* no. 11. New York: Simon & Schuster, 1971, 33–47; and *Writing under Fire,* 196–208.

The narrator is an antiwar activist who confronts the devastating impact of the war at home during the invasion of Cambodia and the killing of four students at Kent State. A shorter, excerpted version of this story is in *Vietnam Voices: Perspectives on the War Years, 1941–1982.* John Clark Pratt, comp. New York: Viking, 1984, 438–40. [_/+/–]

Rottmann, Larry. "Thi Bong Dzu." In *Free Fire Zone,* 119–25; and *Vietnam Anthology,* 50–55.

This story deals with a day in the life of an eleven-year-old Vietcong soldier and the price he pays for taking a few moments out of the war to be a kid. [+]

Shepard, Lucius. "Delta Sly Honey." In *In the Field of Fire,* 24–43.

A troubled soldier who works in Graves Registration finally reaches the point where he goes "outside the wire," to the other side, perhaps dead. When he returns, he is pursued by a patrol of ghost grunts with the radio call sign "Delta Sly Honey."

Stone, Robert. "Helping." In *The Best American Short Stories, 1988.* Mark Helprin, ed., with Shannon Ravenel. Boston: Houghton Mifflin, 1988, 285–313.

A Vietnam veteran has trouble dealing with his fear and anger, and to complicate matters, his wife is having trouble as well. [_/+]

Suddick, Tom. "Caduceus." In *Touring Nam,* 206–21.

After a bloody battle, a squad of Marines finds a way to relieve its tension that involves a rat. [+/–]

———. "A Shithouse Rat." In *Touring Nam,* 325–36.

This is the story of a former Marine who has trouble sleeping at night because of his memories of a particular incident that happened in Vietnam. [_/+/–]

Tavela, John. "The Souvenir." In *Free Fire Zone,* 148–53.

A mess sergeant falls in love with a Vietnamese girl who works in the mess hall. When he asks her to marry him, he makes a discovery that destroys his image of her. [–]

Short Story Collections

Algren, Nelson. *The Last Carousel.* New York: Putnam, 1973.

> A collection of the author's short stories that includes four relating to Vietnam: "I Know They'll Like Me in Saigon," 111–16; "Letter from Saigon," 131–37; "Police and Mama-Sans Get It All," 144–50; and "What Country Do You Think You're In?" 138–43. [+]

Dann, Jeanne Van Buren, and Jack Dann. *In the Field of Fire.* New York: Tor, 1987.

> An anthology of twenty-two science fiction short stories expressing the horror of the Vietnam experience through fantasy. [+]

De Grazia, Emilio. *Enemy Country.* St. Paul, Minn.: New Rivers Press, 1984.

> A collection of eleven short stories on the Vietnam War by the author.

Gulassa, Cyril M. *The Fact of Fiction: Social Relevance in the Short Story.* San Francisco: Canfield Press, 1972.

> Thirty stories that explore universal human problems within the context of today's social problems. Six of the stories deal with Vietnam.

Jenks, Tom. *Soldiers and Civilians: Americans at War and at Home—Short Stories.* New York: Bantam Books, 1986.

> Vietnam is the focus of this collection of nine stories. [+]

Karlin, Wayne, Basil T. Paquet, and Larry Rottmann, eds. *Free Fire Zone: Short Stories by Vietnam Veterans.* New York: McGraw-Hill, 1973.

> A major collection of twenty-six Vietnam short stories. [+/– some stories]

Klinkowitz, Jerome, and John Somer, eds. *Writing under Fire: Stories of the Vietnam War.* New York: Delta, 1978.

> An important collection of twenty stories with a chronology of the war and a bibliography. [+]

Moore, Robin. *Combat Pay.* New York: Manor Books, 1976.

> A collection of twenty-six short stories. Three are about Vietnam: "Combat Pay," 13–41; "We Have Met the Enemy," 181–86; and "Welcome Home." [+]

Anthologies

Anisfield, Nancy, ed. *Vietnam Anthology: American War Literature.* Bowling Green State University Popular Press, 1987.

> An anthology which includes seven novel excerpts, eight short stories, two drama excerpts, and twenty-five poems. Each section has an introduction and study questions. In addition, it includes a time line, statistics, glossary, and bibliography. [+]

Greenberg, Martin H., and Augustus Norton, eds. *Touring Nam: The Vietnam War Reader.* New York: Morrow, 1985.

> An interesting anthology that follows the tour of duty with selections illustrating aspects of life, including arrival in Vietnam, living conditions, first combat, feelings of terror and boredom, and daily life in the jungle. Included are short stories, novel excerpts, and journalistic accounts. [+/–]

Hardy, Gordon, comp. *Words of War: An Anthology of Vietnam War Literature.* Boston: Boston Publishing Company, 1988.

> Volume 24 of *The Vietnam Experience* series is an anthology that excerpts twenty-one novels and personal narratives by major Vietnam War writers. It also includes letters, speeches, newspaper and television editorials, and photographs. [+]

Horne, A. D., ed. *The Wounded Generation: America after Vietnam.* New York: Prentice-Hall, 1981.

> This anthology is intended as a reassessment of the tumultuous events of the Vietnam War viewed from the 1980s. It includes personal narratives, poetry, and novel excerpts from some of the major Vietnam works. [+]

Williams, Reese, ed. *Unwinding the Vietnam War: From War into Peace.* Seattle: Real Comet Press, 1987.

> An anthology of poetry, personal narratives, and critical analyses by veterans, peace activists, and refugees all expressing a need to speak out against the war.

Photography/Art Collections

Anzenberger, Joseph F., Jr., ed. *Combat Art of the Vietnam War.* Jefferson, N.C.: McFarland, 1986.

> This is a fascinating collection of art covering many aspects of the Vietnam conflict. The editor even includes a chapter on humor. [+]

Jury, Mark. *The Vietnam Photo Book.* New York: Grossman, 1971.

Jury was drafted and sent to Vietnam in 1969 where he served as an army photographer. The powerful black-and-white photographs are accompanied by narrations, explanations, and personal accounts.

Lopes, Sal. Conceived. *The Wall: Images and Offerings from the Vietnam Veterans Memorial.* New York: Collins, 1987.

A fascinating and powerful collection of photographs "of the wall and the people who commune there with the dead and the living" by seventeen photojournalists. The collection includes excerpts of letters, notes, and fragments of communication left at the wall by families, friends, and comrades of the 58,132 dead and missing, whose names are engraved there. [+]

Mills, Nick, ed. *Combat Photographer.* Boston: Boston Publishing Company, 1983.

Volume 1 of *The Vietnam Experience* series shows the war, the people, and country of Vietnam as captured on film by combat photographers.

Page, Tim. *Tim Page's Nam.* New York: Knopf, 1983.

A very powerful photographic essay of the war. Page was a British photographer working in Vietnam and was wounded twice while working for *Time-Life.*

Films

Apocalypse Now. Dir. Francis Ford Coppola. United Artists, 1979. (146 minutes, color.) Available through Paramount Home Video.

Frequently compared to Joseph Conrad's *Heart of Darkness,* this is the story of Lieutenant Willard, who receives orders to seek out a renegade military outpost led by the mysterious Colonel Kurtz, and to "terminate his command with extreme prejudice." [_/+/–]

Bat 21. Dir. Peter Markie. Tri-Star, 1988. (112 minutes, color.) Available through Media Home Entertainment.

An American officer is stranded in the wilds of Vietnam, with only one helicopter pilot making sacrifices to try to rescue him. Senior high–adult. [–]

Born on the Fourth of July. Dir. Oliver Stone. Universal Pictures, 1989. (145 minutes, color.) Available through Universal Home Video.

Based on Kovic's book of the same title, the film portrays the life and struggles of disabled Vietnam veteran Ron Kovic. Volunteering to fight for democracy in Vietnam, Kovic endures experiences which alter his perceptions of the war and change his attitudes concerning war and his country. [+/–]

Casualties of War. Dir. Brian De Palma. Columbia Pictures, 1989. (120 minutes, color.) Available through HBO Home Video.

A fact-based account of a twenty-year-old sergeant who supervises the kidnaping, rape, and murder of a peasant girl during a patrol in the jungle. Three members of the unit go along with their sergeant; the fourth is shocked and outraged, though he is unable to do anything to prevent the monstrous attack. [–]

Coming Home. Dir. Hal Ashby. United Artists, 1978. (127 minutes, color.) Available through CBS/Fox Video.

A soldier goes to Vietnam, and while he is gone his wife falls in love with a paraplegic veteran. When the soldier returns from Vietnam, he is a burned-out psychotic, and his wife loyally returns to him, but he soon learns about her affair and turns to violence, the only emotion he can feel. [+]

Dear America: Letters Home from Vietnam. Dir. Bill Couturie. Couturie Co. and Vietnam Veterans Ensemble Theater Company, 1988. (84 minutes, color.) Available through HBO Home Video.

A powerful documentary featuring pictures and film of the war with voice-overs by dozens of Hollywood stars reading the words of American GIs. The film follows a chronology that roughly corresponds to a soldier's year in Vietnam. The readings are from the collection of letters with the same title. Junior high–adult. [+]

The Deer Hunter. Dir. Michael Cimino. Columbia Pictures, 1979. (183 minutes, color.) Available through RCA/Columbia Home Video.

This three-hour movie is a powerful chronicle of the Vietnam War's impact on a small Pennsylvania town. [_/+/–]

84 Charlie MoPic. Dir. Patrick Duncan. The Charlie MoPic Co., 1989. (89 minutes, color.) Available through RCA/Columbia Home Video.

A frighteningly realistic look at jungle combat as seen through the eyes of a six-man recon team. Most of the film was shot with a hand-held camera. Senior high–adult. [+/–]

Full Metal Jacket. Dir. Stanley Kubrick. Warner Brothers, 1987. (117 minutes, color.) Available through Warner Home Video.

Based on the novel *The Short-Timers* by Gustav Hasford, this is the story of a young recruit who is inducted into Marine subculture in boot camp, and then is sent to Vietnam as a combat correspondent where he and an enthusiastic photographer are sent to the front during the 1968 Tet Offensive. They join up with a squad that is part of the force trying to retake the city of Hue from the North Vietnamese Army. The hero and his sidekick experience the horror of the war. For a mature audience. [_/+/–]

Gardens of Stone. Dir. Francis Ford Coppola. Tri-Star Pictures, 1987. (112 minutes, color.) Available through CBS/Fox Video.

A zealous young cadet during the Vietnam War is assigned to the Old Guard patrol at Arlington Cemetery and clashes with the patrol's older officers and various pacifist civilians. Senior high–adult. [–]

Go Tell the Spartans. Dir. Ted Post. United Artists, 1978. (114 minutes, color.) Available through Vestron Video.

Early in the war, 1964, a hard-boiled major is ordered to establish a garrison at Muc Wa with a platoon of burnt-out Americans and Vietnamese mercenaries. [–]

The Green Berets. Dir. John Wayne. Warner Brothers, 1968. (135 minutes, color.) Available through Warner Home Video, Inc.

John Wayne stars as a Special Forces colonel, leading his troops against the Vietcong. Along the way, an antiwar journalist who accompanies the Special Forces unit is gradually won over when he sees the nature of the enemy. Its explicitly prowar bias oversimplifies the nature of the war and U.S. involvement in Vietnam. This film is appropriate for all ages.

Hamburger Hill. Dir. John Irvin. Marcia Nasatir, 1987. (104 minutes, color.) Available through Vestron Video.

This film depicts the famous battle between Americans and VC over a useless hill in Vietnam. [–]

The Hanoi Hilton. Dir. Lionel Chetwynd. Cannon Films, 1987. (126 minutes, color.) Available through Warner Home Video.

This is a brutal drama following the sufferings of American POWs in Vietnamese prison camps. Senior high–adult. [–]

Hearts and Minds. Dir. Peter Davis. Touchstone, 1974. (112 minutes, color.) Available through Paramount Home Video.

This Academy Award-winning documentary is a gripping account of America's misguided involvement in Vietnam. Senior high–adult. [+]

In Country. Dir. Norman Jewison. Warner Brothers, 1988. (116 minutes, color.) Available through Warner Home Video.

> Based on Bobbie Ann Mason's novel *In Country,* this film tells the story of seventeen-year-old Samantha Hughes's quest to understand the torments of Vietnam and the effect the war had on the people closest in her life. Sam's father died in the war; this makes her try to understand the legacy of Vietnam all the more through her eccentric Uncle Emmet and other local veterans who are still haunted by the war. Eventually her quest takes her to the Vietnam Veterans Memorial in Washington, D.C. [+]

Jacknife. Dir. David Jones, Kings Road Entertainment, 1989. (102 minutes, color.) Available through HBO Video.

> Based on Stephen Metcalfe's play *Strange Snow,* this is the story of two Vietnam veterans haunted by memories of the war. [+]

Jacob's Ladder. Dir. Adrian Lyne. Carolco Home Video, 1990. (116 minutes, color.) Available through Live Home Video.

> A psychological thriller involving a Vietnam veteran, Jacob Singer, who was wounded in the war. Torn between memories of his son and terrifying wartime demons, he is drawn into a web of intrigue by his girlfriend and begins to lose his grip on reality. Jacob must confront his memories. [–]

The Killing Fields. Dir. Roland Joffe. Warner Brothers, 1984. (142 minutes, color.) Available through Warner Home Video.

> Based on the book *The Death and Life of Dith Pran* by Sydney H. Schanberg, this is the story of Dith, who is Schanberg's Cambodian aide, translator, and friend. Dith saves Schanberg and other Western correspondents from execution when the Khmer Rouge capture the Cambodian capital in 1975. But the men he saves cannot in turn save him. Dith is exiled to countryside labor camps, where he endures four years of starvation, torture, and war before escaping to neighboring Thailand. [+/–]

The Odd Angry Shot. Dir. Tom Jeffrey. Atlantic Television Inc./Samson Productions, 1979. (92 minutes, color.) Available through Vestron Video.

> An interesting Australian film that follows a scout team of Australian soldiers from its send-off at home to its return from Vietnam. The film explores the horrors of combat and the deterioration of the men as the war drags on. [+/–]

Platoon. Dir. Oliver Stone. Hemdale Film Corporation, 1986. (120 minutes, color.) Available through HBO Home Video.

This is an intense drama that examines the fight between good and evil among an American infantry rifle platoon in the jungles of Vietnam. [+/–]

Streamers. Dir. Robert Altman. MGM/United Artists, 1984. (119 minutes, color.) Available through Media Home Entertainment.

Based on the play by David Rabe, this is the story of a group of young soldiers in a claustrophobic army barracks tensely awaiting the orders that will send the soldiers to Vietnam. Senior high–adult.

Vietnam: A Television History. Prod. WGBH Boston, 1983. (60 minutes each, color.) Available through Films, Inc.; Sony Video software.

This series of thirteen one-hour programs looks at Vietnam from the 1945 revolution against the French to the U.S. evacuation of Saigon in 1975. Very useful for providing background and history to help students understand the context of the literature. Senior high–adult. [+]

Vietnam: The Ten Thousand Day War. Prod. Michael Maclear, 1980. (49 minutes each, color.) Available through Nelson Entertainment.

This series of thirteen programs examines the emotional and physical impact of the Vietnam War on the men who fought in it. It provides excellent background material to help students understand the literature. Senior high–adult. [+]

Vietnam: The War at Home. Prod. Catalyst Media; Glen Silver, 1978. (100 minutes, color.) Available through MPI Home Video.

This acclaimed documentary uses a wide array of news and interview footage to examine the effects of the Vietnam political ambiguities on the home front. It concentrates on student activists at the University of Wisconsin. It was nominated for the Best Documentary Oscar. Junior high–adult. [+]

Vietnam War Story II. Prod. HBO Pictures, 1988. (90 minutes, color.) Available through HBO Home Video.

Three short, made-for-TV war stories (each is thirty minutes long) set in Vietnam: "An Old Ghost Walks the Earth," "R&R," and "The Fragging." The stories are supposedly based on the actual experiences of Vietnam veterans. Each story focuses on a single theme. Junior high–adult. [+]

Vietnam War Story III. Prod. HBO Pictures, 1989. (90 minutes, color.)

Three short, made-for-TV war stories (each is 30 minutes long) set in Vietnam: "Separated," "Dusk to Dawn," and "The Promise." Based on the actual experiences of Vietnam veterans, each story focuses on a single theme. Junior high–adult. [+]

Works Cited

Anisfield, Nancy. "Words and Fragments: Narrative Style in Vietnam War Novels." In *Search and Clear: Critical Responses to Selected Literature and Films of the Vietnam War,* ed. William J. Searle, 56–61. Bowling Green, Ohio: Bowling Green State University Popular Press, 1988.

Baker, Mark. *Nam: The Vietnam War in the Words of the Men and Women Who Fought There.* New York: Morrow, 1981.

Beidler, Philip D. *American Literature and the Experience of Vietnam.* Athens: University of Georgia Press, 1982.

Bryan, C.D.B. "Barely Suppressed Screams: Getting a Bead on Vietnam War Literature." *Harper's* 268 (June 1984): 67–72.

Caputo, Philip. *A Rumor of War.* New York: Holt, Rinehart & Winston, 1977.

Carter, Candy. "The Vietnam War and Era in the English Classroom." In *Whole Language Catalog,* eds. Kenneth S. Goodman, Lois Bridges Bird, and Yetta M. Goodman, 292. Santa Rosa, Cal.: American School Publishers, 1991.

———. "Vietnam War Literature." Paper presented at the annual spring conference of the National Council of Teachers of English, Charleston, S.C., 6–8 April 1989.

Christie, N. Bradley. "Teaching Our Longest War: Constructive Lessons from Vietnam." *English Journal* 78 (April 1989): 35–38.

Cohen, Steven. "Vietnam in the Classroom." *Social Education* 52 (January 1988): 47–48.

Cussler, Elizabeth B. "Vietnam: An Oral History." *English Journal* 76 (November 1987): 66–67.

DallaGrana, Wade. "Vietnam in the High School Curriculum." *Social Education* 52 (January 1988): 49–50.

Doherty, Thomas. "Full Metal Genre: Stanley Kubrick's Vietnam Combat Movie." *Film Quarterly* 42 (Winter 1988): 24–30.

Ehrhart, W. D. "Why Teach Vietnam?" *Social Education* 52 (January 1988): 25–26.

Endress, William Bliss. "Teaching Vietnam: Reflections Beyond the Immediate." *English Journal* 73 (December 1984): 28–39.

Farish, Terry. "If You Knew Him, Please Write Me: Novels about the War in Vietnam." *School Library Journal* 35 (November 1988): 52–53.

Farrell, Edmund J. "Oral Histories as Living Literature." *English Journal* 71 (April 1982): 87–92.

Fernekes, William R. "Student Inquiries about the Vietnam War." *Social Education* 52 (January 1988): 53–54.

Freedman, Samuel G. "The War and the Arts." *New York Times Magazine,* 31 March 1985: 50+.

Gilman, Owen. "Vietnam and the Paradoxical Paradigm of Nomenclature." In *Search and Clear: Critical Responses to Selected Literature and Films of the Vietnam War,* ed. William J. Searle, 62–73. Bowling Green, Ohio: Bowling Green State University Popular Press, 1988.

Glassman, Joel. "Teaching Students and Ourselves about the Vietnam War." *Social Education* 52 (January 1988): 35–36.

Goldstein, Jonathan. "Using Literature in a Course on the Vietnam War." *College Teaching* 37 (March 1989): 91–95.

Goodman, Allan. "Scholars Must Give More Serious Thought to How They Teach and Write about the War in Vietnam." *The Chronicle of Higher Education,* 25 July 1990: A36.

Hellmann, John. *American Myth and the Legacy of Vietnam.* New York: Columbia University Press, 1989.

Herr, Michael. *Dispatches.* New York: Avon Books, 1978.

Herzog, Tobey C. "John Wayne in a Modern Heart of Darkness: The American Soldier in Vietnam." In *Search and Clear: Critical Responses to Selected Literature and Films of the Vietnam War,* ed. William J. Searle, 16–25. Bowling Green, Ohio: Bowling Green State University Popular Press, 1988.

———. "Writing about Vietnam: A Heavy Heart-of-Darkness Trip." *College English* 41 (February 1980): 680–95.

Johannessen, Larry R. "Vietnam in the English Classroom." Paper presented at the annual spring conference of the National Council of Teachers of English, Charleston, S.C., 6–8 April 1989 (ERIC Document Reproduction Service No. ED 310 407).

———. "Teaching the Vietnam War: Two Short Stories." *NOTES Plus 8* (September 1990): 12–15.

Johannessen, Larry R., Elizabeth A. Kahn, and Carolyn Calhoun Walter. "The Art of Introducing Literature." *The Clearing House* 57 (1984): 263–66.

Just, Ward. "Vietnam: The Camera Lies." *Atlantic Monthly* (December 1979): 63–65.

Kirschner, George, and Eric Welsberg. "Teaching and Learning about the Vietnam War." *Social Education* 52 (January 1988): 51–52.

Kahn, Elizabeth A., Carolyn Calhoun Walter, and Larry R. Johannessen. *Writing about Literature.* Urbana, Ill.: ERIC/NCTE, 1984.

Lawson, Jacqueline E. "'Old Kids': The Adolescent Experience in the Nonfiction Narratives of the Vietnam War." In *Search and Clear: Critical Responses to Selected Literature and Films of the Vietnam War,* ed. William J. Searle, 26–36. Bowling Green, Ohio: Bowling Green State University Popular Press, 1988.

Lloyd-Jones, Richard, and Andrea A. Lunsford. *The English Coalition Conference: Democracy through Language.* Urbana, Ill.: NCTE/MLA, 1989.

Lowry, Timothy S. *And Brave Men, Too.* New York: Crown, 1985.

Lomperis, Timothy J. *"Reading the Wind": The Literature of the Vietnam War—An Interpretive Critique.* Durham, N.C.: Duke University Press, 1987.

MacPherson, Myra. *Long Time Passing: Vietnam and the Haunted Generation.* New York: Doubleday, 1984.

Mandel, Norma H. "The Use of the Novel to Discuss Vietnamese Refugee Experiences." *English Journal* 77 (April 1988): 40–44.

Matlaw, Martha. "Teaching the Vietnam War at Full Circle High School." *Social Education* 52 (January 1988): 44–46.

Myers, Thomas. *Walking Point: American Narratives of Vietnam.* New York: Oxford University Press, 1988.

Naparsteck, Martin J. "The Vietnam War Novel." *Humanist* 39 (July 1979): 37–39.

O'Brien, Tim. "How to Tell a True War Story." *Esquire* 108 (October 1987): 208–15.

Oldham, Perry. "On Teaching Vietnam War Literature." *English Journal* 75 (February 1986): 55–56.

Paris, Michael. "The American Film Industry & Vietnam." *History Today* 37 (April 1987): 19–26.

Pratt, John Clark. "Bibliographic Commentary: 'From the Fiction, Some Truths.'" In *"Reading the Wind": The Literature of the Vietnam War—An Interpretive Critique,* by Timothy J. Lomperis, 115–63. Durham, N.C.: Duke University Press, 1987.

Rosenblatt, Louise M. *Literature as Exploration.* New York: Noble and Noble, 1968.

Searle, William J. "Introduction." In *Search and Clear: Critical Responses to Selected Literature and Films of the Vietnam War,* ed. William J. Searle, 1–13. Bowling Green, Ohio: Bowling Green State University Popular Press, 1988.

Searle, William J., ed. *Search and Clear: Critical Responses to Selected Literature and Films of the Vietnam War.* Bowling Green, Ohio: Bowling Green State University Popular Press, 1988.

Smagorinsky, Peter. *Expressions: Multiple Intelligences in the English Class.* Urbana, Ill.: National Council of Teachers of English, 1991.

Smagorinsky, Peter, and Steven Gevinson. *Fostering the Reader's Response: Rethinking the Literature Curriculum.* Palo Alto, Cal.: Dale Seymour, 1989.

Smagorinsky, Peter, Tom McCann, and Steven Kern. *Explorations: Introductory Activities for Literature and Composition, 7–12.* Urbana, Ill.: ERIC/NCTE, 1987.

Smith, Michael W., and George Hillocks, Jr. "Sensible Sequencing: Developing Knowledge about Literature Text by Text." *English Journal* 77 (October 1988): 44–49.

Starr, Jerold M. "The Making of the Lessons of the Vietnam War." *Social Education* 52 (January 1988b): 29–32.

———. "Teaching the Vietnam War." *Social Education* 52 (January 1988a): 23–24.

Walsh, Jeffrey. *American War Literature: 1914 to Vietnam.* New York: St. Martin's Press, 1982.

Whitteman, Paul A. "Vietnam: 15 Years Later." *Time,* 30 April 1990: 18–29.

Wilcox, Fred A. "Pedagogical Implications of Teaching 'Literature of the Vietnam War.'" *Social Education* 52 (January 1988): 39–40.

Wittman, Sandra M. *Writing about Vietnam: A Bibliography of the Literature of the Vietnam Conflict.* Boston: G. K. Hall, 1989.

"Young Adult Choices." *Journal of Reading* 34 (1990): 203–09.

Appendix

1 Vietnam War Opinionnaire

Directions: Read each of the following statements. Write *A* if you agree with the statement or *D* if you disagree with it.

Agree or
Disagree

_____ 1. "The only heroes in war are the dead ones."

_____ 2. "My country right or wrong" is not just a slogan—it is every citizen's patriotic duty.

_____ 3. Rambo is a good image for Americans to have of the Vietnam veteran: he represents all that America stands for and the American soldier in war.

_____ 4. No cause, political or otherwise, is worth dying for.

_____ 5. Most American soldiers participated in acts of brutality against Vietnamese civilians.

_____ 6. "Ask not what your country can do for you—ask what you can do for your country."

_____ 7. It is never right to kill another person.

_____ 8. The men who fought in the Vietnam War did so because they were very patriotic.

_____ 9. Movies like *Rambo* are very bad because they show a distorted view of what war is really like and of what it is like to be a soldier.

_____ 10. "The soldier, above all other people, prays for peace, for he must suffer and bear the deepest wounds and scars of war."

_____ 11. The Vietnam War was a guerrilla war; therefore, it is understandable that Vietnamese civilians suffered as a result of American military actions.

_____ 12. People should never compromise their ideals or beliefs.

_____ 13. For soldiers who served in Vietnam, the difference between death and survival often meant not worrying about potential harm to innocent civilians or doing the right or moral thing.

_____ 14. When Vietnam veterans came home from the war, most Americans treated them as returning heroes.

Illumination Rounds by Larry R. Johannessen © 1992 NCTE.

2 Patriotism, Protest, and War Opinionnaire

Directions: In the space provided indicate whether you agree or disagree with each statement. Be prepared to explain your answers.

Agree or
Disagree

_____ 1. "Cowards die many times before their deaths; the valiant taste of death but once."

_____ 2. It is never right to kill another person.

_____ 3. People should never compromise their ideals or beliefs.

_____ 4. In time of war, people have to make sacrifices.

_____ 5. Rambo is a good image for Americans to have of the American war veteran; he represents all that America stands for and the American soldier in war.

_____ 6. Women have very little to do with war; they do not fight and suffer very little.

_____ 7. "The men who do well on the average, perhaps with one moment of glory, those men are brave."

_____ 8. Most American soldiers in the Vietnam War participated in acts of brutality against Vietnamese civilians.

_____ 9. No cause, political or otherwise, is worth dying for.

_____ 10. "The soldier, above all other people, prays for peace, for he must suffer and bear the deepest wounds and scars of war."

_____ 11. "My country right or wrong" is not just a slogan—it is every citizen's patriotic duty.

_____ 12. Movies like *Rambo* are very bad because they show a distorted view of what war is really like and of what it is like to be a soldier.

_____ 13. Any American soldier who refuses to fight or who deserts in war should be shot for being a coward and a traitor.

_____ 14. The men who fought in America's wars did so because they were very patriotic.

_____ 15. "The only heroes in war are the dead ones."

_____ 16. Those who avoid the draft or desert and go to some other country should never be given amnesty or allowed to return to the United States.

_____ 17. Rarely in any of America's wars have American soldiers participated in acts of brutality against civilians or others.

_____ 18. Which war among those listed below was the worst war America has ever been involved in? (Circle one.)

   a. Revolutionary War

   b. Civil War

   c. World War I

   d. World War II

   e. Korean War

   f. Vietnam War

3 Heroism: What Is a Heroic Act?

Rank the following actions from the one you think is the MOST heroic to the one you think is the LEAST heroic. Be prepared to explain your reasons for ranking each action as you did.

1	2	3	4	5	6	7	8	9	10

Most   Least

A. A woman is swimming in the ocean. Sharks are spotted near her, so her husband runs into the water to save her. Part of his leg is severed by sharks, but he manages to pull his wife and himself to safety.

B. A scientist makes a discovery that will help cure thousands of people with heart disease.

C. An accident leaves a gymnast paralyzed. For five years she spends 12 to 14 hours a day in therapy to try to regain the use of her legs. Her hard work results in a miraculous recovery, and she wins a gold medal in the Olympics.

D. A man runs into a burning building that is about to collapse to rescue a child trapped inside. As he is running out with the child, a portion of the building falls, killing them both.

E. When a boat capsizes in a storm, four people are clinging to a small raft that will hold only three. An old man with a fatal disease knows he will die in a few months, so he gives up the raft for the others. He drowns in the waves.

F. A school teacher, invited to be a part of the seven-person crew of the Space Shuttle, dies as the rocket explodes shortly after takeoff.

G. A bystander helps a woman who is drowning in the river after a plane crash. The water is very cold, and only a few minutes of exposure could result in death. He is able to save the woman but freezes and drowns in the process.

H. An 11-year-old boy who sees two men sexually assaulting a 13-year-old girl, threatening to stab her if she resists, rides off on his bicycle and gets the police. The officers arrive too late to prevent the rape, but the boy's actions probably prevent her from being killed.

I. A lifeguard rescues a six-year-old boy from drowning in a public pool by dragging him out with a hook.

J. A man finds that the company he works for has been cheating customers. He reports his finding on a television news program. Shortly thereafter, he is fired from his job.

Illumination Rounds by Larry R. Johannessen © 1992 NCTE.

4 Operation Search

Directions: Select one of the following topics, and then using facts and other information you gather in the library, prepare and give an oral presentation. You must use at least one poster in your presentation to help explain your topic. The drawings, photographs, or maps on your poster should have captions that explain the meaning of the visual presentations.

Vietnam War Research Topics

1. The Gulf of Tonkin Incident and Resolution
2. The Early Years: 1955–1964
3. LBJ Goes to War: 1964–1968
4. Nixon's War: 1969–1973
5. The Paris Peace Talks/Agreement
6. The Fall of South Vietnam
7. The Kent State University Shootings
8. Daniel Ellsberg and the Pentagon Papers
9. French Colonialism in Vietnam
10. The Battle of Dienbienphu
11. Ho Chi Minh
12. History of Vietnam
13. Geography of Vietnam and Southeast Asia
14. Vietnam: Culture and Customs
15. Vietnam: Art and Literature
16. Vietnam: Religion and Philosophy
17. Draft Dodgers, Evaders, and Avoiders
18. Tom Hayden and the SDS (Students for a Democratic Society)
19. VVAW (Vietnam Veterans Against the War)
20. Military Deserters
21. The Draft
22. Women Who Served in Vietnam
23. Antiwar Movement

24. The Tet Offensive of 1968

25. The Siege of Khe Sahn

26. The Battle of Hue

27. The My Lai Massacre

28. The Ho Chi Minh Trail

29. The National Liberation Front (Vietcong)

30. The North Vietnamese Army (NVA)

31. The Secret War in Cambodia and Laos

32. The Army of the Republic of Vietnam (South Vietnam)

33. The Invasion of Cambodia

34. Agent Orange

35. Posttraumatic Stress Disorder

36. Vietnamese Refugees—Boat People

37. POWs/MIAs

38. The Vietnam Veterans Memorial, Washington, D.C.

39. The Antiwar Movement on College Campuses

40. Conscientious Objectors

41. Jane Fonda and the Antiwar Movement

Illumination Rounds by Larry R. Johannessen © 1992 NCTE.

5 Vietnam and the Arts

Directions: Select one of the following topics, and then using the information you gather, prepare and give an oral presentation that answers the questions posed in your topic. In your presentation, you must show the art, photography, or other visual works, or play the music that is the focus of your report.

1. The protest songs of the 1960s reflect events that were taking place. How do these songs reflect the political controversies over the Vietnam War? How is this music reflected in the literature of the Vietnam War? Which songs and/or artists seem to be most important? Why?

2. Many rock-and-roll songs were popular with GIs who fought in Vietnam. Which rock-and-roll songs and/or artists were most popular with those who served in Vietnam? Why? How is this music reflected in Vietnam War literature? How does this music reflect the political controversies of the time?

3. In the 1960s and early 1970s artists began depicting the war in Vietnam. How do artists like Peter Saul and others portray the Vietnam War? How do these works reflect the political controversies of the time? Which artists and/or works of art seem to be most important? Why? How are these portrayals of the war reflected in Vietnam War literature?

4. Magazines, newspapers, and television brought images of the war into American homes on a daily basis. Some of these images became touchstones for the growing unrest at home over the war. How did television news cameras and photographers portray the war in Vietnam? Which images were most important in terms of the political controversies of the time? How are these images reflected in the literature of the Vietnam War?

5. Classical music was also influenced by the war in Vietnam. The music of Leonard Bernstein and Richard Wernick are two notable examples. How does this music reflect the political controversies of the time? Which music and/or artists seem to be most important and why? How is this music or the themes in this music reflected in the literature of the Vietnam War?

6. Dance was not exempt from the Vietnam War. Yvonne Rainer and others were influenced by the war. How did dance reflect the issues surrounding the Vietnam War? Which artists seem to be most important and why? How are the themes of dance reflected in the literature of the war?

7. As early as 1972, some pop music began to deal with a new issue, the Vietnam veteran. How is this issue reflected in the music of artists like Marvin Gaye and Curtis Mayfield, and how is this subject treated in pop music of the 1980s? How is this music reflected in the literature of the Vietnam War? How does it reflect changing attitudes toward the war and Vietnam veterans? Which artists and/or music seem most important in terms of this issue? Why?

8. The visual art produced by combat artists during the war and that produced by Vietnam veterans depict the war and its aftermath in striking ways. How does this art depict the war and its aftermath? Which works and/or artists seem most important? Why? How are these views of the war reflected in the literature? How do they reflect the controversies or issues of the time or changing attitudes toward the war?

9. Popular music in the 1980s illustrates new attitudes toward and views of the Vietnam War and those who served in the war. How does this music see the war in Vietnam and the Vietnam veteran? Which songs and/or artists seem most important in this regard? Why? How does this music reflect the change in attitudes and views in society? How is this music reflected in the literature of the Vietnam War?

10. The Vietnam Veterans Memorial in Washington, D.C., has been called everything from the "black ditch" to a powerful work of art. How does this memorial reflect the lingering wounds of the Vietnam War? What is your assessment of this memorial? Is it a "black gash of shame" or a work of art that has the potential to help heal the wounds of the war? How is the controversy over the memorial and/or the meaning of the memorial reflected in the literature of the Vietnam War?

Illumination Rounds by Larry R. Johannessen © 1992 NCTE.

6 Burning Tracer: Interpreting a Vietnam War Poem

Fragment: 5 September 1967

We lay in mud, struggling
While the waves of earth broke over us,
Swallowed us,
And cast us loose on a sea of madness.

Eighteen—
And the blood felt like tears
On the blade of my bayonet;

And youthful dreams lay dead
Amid spent cartridges and broken bodies
Littering the earth.
After that, there was no innocence;
And there was no future to believe in.

—W. D. Ehrhart

1. Define each of these words:

   a. fragment

   b. bayonet

   c. spent cartridges

2. What event is the speaker of the poem describing?

3. What is this event compared to in the first stanza?

4. What is the effect of this event on the speaker?

5. What comparisons does the poet use to show the effect of this event?

6. State the comment or generalization the poem makes about war. Give specific evidence to support your conclusions.

7 Burning Tracers: Vietnam War Poems

Directions: Read each of the following poems carefully and be sure to look up words you do not know. For each poem, write a statement of the poet's generalization about war. In other words, explain the comment the poem makes about the Vietnam War. Be prepared to offer specific evidence that supports your interpretations.

The Man In Black

The man in black
Ran from us
Into a hedgerow
And was gone.
Our small,
Spinning bullets followed,
But did not find him.

We walked
Among the corn and cane,
Wanting to run.

We walked
On line,
Urging one another
To move on
Against our visions
Of torn flesh and smashed bone.

We walked
Among the hootches,
Smelling the greasy smoke
From fires cooking rice and fish;
Wondering, wildly,
Where the man in black was hiding.

On the other side of the village,
We found
The man in black,
As he rose
From his mud bunker
To send three
        quick
                bullets
Through Harry.

And then all our fear
    and hate
Poured from our rifles
Into

    the man in black;
As he lost his face
In the smoke
of an exploding hand frag.*

    —Frank A. Cross, Jr.

*frag: a fragmentation grenade.

APO 96225*

A young man once went off to war
in a far country
When he had time, he wrote home and
said, "Sure rains here a lot."

But his mother, reading between the lines,
Wrote, "We're quite concerned. Tell us
What it's really like."

And the young man responded, "Wow, you ought
to see the funny monkeys!"

To which the mother replied, "Don't
hold back, how is it?"

And the young man wrote, "The sunsets here
are spectacular."

In her next letter the mother
wrote, "Son we want you to tell us
everything."

So the next time he wrote,
"Today I killed a man.
Yesterday I helped drop napalm on women and
children. Tomorrow we are going to use
gas."

And the father wrote, "Please don't
write such depressing letters. You're upsetting
your mother."

So, after a while, the young man wrote, "Sure rains
a lot here. . . ."

    —Larry Rottmann

*APO 96225: Army Post Office for Army personnel serving in Vietnam.

The Insert

Our view of sky, jungle and fields constricts
Into a sink hole covered with saw-grass

Undulating, soon whipped slant as the chopper
Hovers at four feet. Rapt, boot deep in slime,

We deploy ourself in loose perimeter,
listening for incoming rockets above

The thump of rotor blades; edgy for contact,
Junkies of terror impatient to shoot up.

Nothing moves, nothing sounds; then, single file,
We move across a stream-bed toward high ground.

The terror of the insert's quickly over.
Too quickly . . . And more quickly every time . . .

       —R. L. Barth

Corporal Charles Chungtu, U.S.M.C.

This is what the war ended up being about:
we would find a V.C. village,
and if we could not capture it
or clear it of Cong,
we called for jets.
The jets would come in, low and terrible,
sweeping down, and screaming,
in their first pass over the village.
Then they would return, dropping their first bombs
that flattened the huts to rubble and debris.
And then the jets would sweep back again
and drop more bombs
that blew the rubble and debris
to dust and ashes.
And then the jets would come back once again,
in a last pass, this time to drop napalm
that burned the dust and ashes to just nothing.
Then the village
that was not a village any more
was our village.

       —Bryan Alec Floyd

Illumination Rounds by Larry R. Johannessen © 1992 NCTE.

8 Interpreting a Vietnam War Poem

Read the following poem and write a composition in which you (1) explain the generalization or comment the poem makes about the Vietnam War and (2) explain, through effective use of evidence from the poem, the reasons for your interpretation of the poem's meaning.

Coming Home

San Francisco airport—

No more corpsmen stuffing ruptured chests
with cotton balls and not enough heat tabs
to eat a decent meal.

I asked some girl to sit
and have a Coke with me.
She thought I was crazy.
I thought she was going to call a cop.

I bought a ticket for Philadelphia.
At the loading gate, they told me:
"Thank you for flying TWA;
we hope you will enjoy your flight."
No brass bands;
no flags,
no girls,
no cameramen.
Only a small boy who asked me
what the ribbons on my jacket meant.

    —W. D. Ehrhart

Illumination Rounds by Larry R. Johannessen © 1992 NCTE.

9 "Night March" by Tim O'Brien Discussion Questions

1. How long has Paul Berlin been in Vietnam?

2. What happened in the afternoon that has Paul worried?

3. What kind of person is Paul? Is he intelligent or stupid? Strong or weak? How old do you think he is? What evidence leads you to your conclusions?

4. What things does Paul imagine? Why does he dream up so many scenes and conversations?

5. What is it like to be on a night march in Vietnam? What details lead to your conclusions?

6. What is so unusual or surprising about what happened to Billy Boy?

7. What kind of person is Buff? Why does he say he'd shoot Paul for sleeping? Do you think he really would have? Why or why not? Why does he smother Paul's giggling?

8. What fears does Paul have? How does he describe his fears?

9. Why can't Paul stop giggling? What is O'Brien saying about fear? What can a soldier do to try to overcome fear?

10. How is Paul different at the end of the story from the way he was at the beginning? Explain.

Illumination Rounds by Larry R. Johannessen © 1992 NCTE.

10 Vietnam Lexicon

The Vietnam War produced its own unique language which has become part of its literature. In order to understand the literature and the war, you need to understand this language. It consists of a combination of Americanized foreign words and phrases, military jargon, rock music lyrics, and a unique in-country vocabulary derived from various sources.

Americanized Foreign Words and Phrases

boo-coo: many (perversion of the French *beaucoup,* passed down to Americans by Vietnamese, who learned it from the French).

dee-dee (also *dee-dee mau* [Vietnamese *didi*—to run]): get out of here.

dinky dau (Vietnamese *dien cai dau*): to be crazy.

gook: Korean slang for "person," passed down by Korean War veterans and others who served in Korea. Generic term for Oriental person, especially the enemy. Also, "gooner."

mamasan: slang word consisting of the American word "mama," meaning mother, and the Japanese "san," meaning old or respected one; used by GIs referring to older Asian women.

tee-tee (Vietnamese *ti ti*): very small.

Military Jargon

alpha: the military phonetic for the letter A.

bouncing betty: a land mine that when triggered, pops up waist high and sprays shrapnel.

Charlie: the military phonetic for the letter C; also, the Viet Cong; also, variants along the lines of "Mr. Charles" and "Mr. Charlie."

chopper: helicopter.

frag: a fragmentation hand grenade (to frag: to try to kill or wound a
    fellow soldier using a grenade).

gunship: heavily armed helicopter used to support infantry troops.

KIA: killed in action.

LRRP or LURP: long-range reconnaissance patrol.

LZ: helicopter landing zone.

M-16: automatic/semiautomatic assault rifle.

medevac: medical evacuation by helicopter.

perimeter: fortified boundary protecting a position.

RPG: rocket-propelled grenade.

VC: Vietcong; soldiers of the National Liberation Front.

Rock Music Lyrics

Puff the Magic Dragon: C-47 cargo plane mounted with 7.62 mm ma-
    chine guns.

Spooky/The Spook: another name for the C-47 cargo plane mounted
    with 7.62 mm machine guns.

rock'n'roll: firing a weapon on full automatic.

In-Country Vocabulary

cherry: new recruit.

dink: derogatory term for the Vietnamese.

get some: a common exhortation to kill the enemy.

honcho: chief; boss.

hootch/hooch: any small hut, office, or building.

"It don't mean nothin'": the soldier's standard response to anything negative that happens; used as a way to cope with difficult situations.

lifer: a career military person.

no sweat: easy, can do.

number one: the best.

short-timer: a person with a short time left to serve in Vietnam.

The World: the United States.

wasted: killed.

zapped: killed.

11 "With the Enemy" Discussion Questions

1. How are Bung's and Dzu's descriptions of Americans and military equipment different from the way an American would describe them?

2. Were you surprised to learn that Bung was a Vietcong? How did this change your opinion of him?

3. Were you surprised to learn that Dzu was only eleven years old? How did this change your view of him?

4. What surprised you about Mister Hawkins? What are his main concerns? Why is he unable to understand those around him?

5. What surprised you about Sergeant Tree? What are his main concerns? Why is he unable to understand those around him?

6. According to these two stories, how would you describe the Vietnamese people? How are they different from Americans?

7. Which Vietnamese people in these stories do you feel empathy for? Why? Which Vietnamese people in these stories do you not feel empathy for? Why not?

8. What are Huddle and Rottmann saying about the Vietnam War?

Illumination Rounds by Larry R. Johannessen © 1992 NCTE.

12 The War at Home: Short Story Chart

Story/Main characters	War-related events described	Effects of war on individuals, families, and society
Fish Narrator Karen	Invasion of Cambodia Shootings at Kent State	Strain on relationship; realization of possible death; doubts about protesting the war; fragmentation of self; destruction of society; killing on the streets of U.S.A.; if we survive, women will be stronger, men will be beautiful because we protested the madness of the war

Story 2: _____

Story 3: _____

Story 4: _____

Story 5: _____

Illumination Rounds by Larry R. Johannessen © 1992 NCTE.

13 Some Themes from *Dear America: Letters Home from Vietnam*

1. Without a clear purpose in Vietnam, killing the enemy became the only goal.

   a. "Our mission is to find VC and kill them."

   b. _____

   _____

2. The killing became easy and soldiers became callous and even cruel.

   a. "Instead of a yellow streak, you got a mean streak."

   b. _____

   _____

3. The many frustrations, the terror, the death and destruction, the young age of most of the soldiers, the lack of clear purpose, all seemed to produce a kind of insanity.

   a. "They're just kids, 18, 19. I got to get out of here."

   b. For awhile when I read your letters, I'm a normal person again."

   c. _____

   _____

4. _____

   _____

   a. "Move without contact. We are all scared. The VC are all around us."

   b. "The night belongs to Charlie."

c. _____
_____
_____

d. _____
_____
_____

5. _____
_____
_____

a. _____
_____
_____

b. _____
_____
_____

c. _____
_____
_____

14 Responding to *Dear America: Letters Home from Vietnam*

Select one of the following topics on *Dear America: Letters Home from Vietnam* and write a short essay that answers the questions given in the topic you select.

Topic A: Movie critics have described the film as "a wrenching experience. . . . You're not likely to find a more moving movie experience on any screen." What things (at least two) struck you the most about the film? Why? What kind of impact did they have? Be as specific as you can in describing the images, words, and/or ideas that had an impact on you and why they struck you.

Topic B: While the film never becomes a praise of the war in Southeast Asia, it does become a kind of tribute to the men and women who had to fight in Vietnam. In what ways (at least two) does the film pay tribute to the men and women who served in Vietnam? Be specific in identifying the ways and in presenting examples (images, words, and/or ideas) that illustrate these ways.

Topic C: One film critic has said, "What the men and women in Vietnam felt and saw takes on a disturbing reality all its own and becomes a poignant appeal for peace. Yes, an eloquent cry for peace." How is the film an appeal for peace (at least two ways)? Be specific in identifying how the film is an appeal for peace and in presenting examples (images, words and/or ideas) that illustrate these ways.

15 Thinking about *Vietnam: The War at Home*

Select one of the following topics on *Vietnam: The War at Home* and write a short composition that answers the questions in the topic you are writing about.

1. **Words and Images:** Think about the words and images that made the strongest impressions on you. Which statement from the film made the strongest impression on you? Why? What do you feel and think about it? Which image from the film made the strongest impression on you? Why? What do you feel and think about it?

2. **Questions:** To what extent did the film confirm or contradict your own views on the war? In what ways did it confirm or contradict your own views? What questions or problems did the film raise for you? What more would you like to know?

3. **War and Morality:** This film raises serious questions about the "rightness" or morality of the Vietnam War. Was the war in Vietnam right? Why or why not? If not, under what circumstances would you risk your life in combat for the sake of the nation? If so, under what circumstances might you refuse to risk your life in combat for the sake of the nation?

4. **The Costs of War:** This film asks us to think about the costs and consequences of the Vietnam War. Which of these do you think are most serious and/or long-range? Why? What can we do to overcome them?

Illumination Rounds by Larry R. Johannessen © 1992 NCTE.

16 Independent Reading Questions: *If I Die in a Combat Zone* by Tim O'Brien

1. Describe the author's background and maturation before he joined the military.

2. O'Brien is opposed to the war. Why doesn't he desert or go to Canada? What keeps him from doing this?

3. Describe Basic Training and Advanced Infantry Training (AIT) and how O'Brien and his friend Erik dealt with it.

4. Describe O'Brien's arrival in Vietnam and his reaction to his arrival.

5. Give examples from this book of the following:

   a. Terror in battle

   b. Courage in battle

   c. Confusion over who was the enemy

   d. Admirable officers

   e. Incompetent officers

   f. War atrocities (on both sides)

   g. War technology

   h. Life away from the combat zone

   i. The ancient rules of warfare

Analysis

6. There is some thought that war is a rite of passage for males in our society. To what extent does this book prove or disprove that theory?

7. What does O'Brien say about the wisdom of the Vietnam War?
    You might want to consider what he has to say on page 130: "It is
    not a war fought for territory, nor for pieces of land that will be
    won and held. It is not a war fought to win the hearts of the Viet-
    namese nationals, not in the wake of the contempt drawn on our
    faces and on theirs, not in the wake of a burning village, a
    trampled rice paddy, a battered detainee . . . ."

8. What does O'Brien have to say about courage? You might con-
    sider the following passage on page 141: "Men must know what
    they do is courageous, they must know it is right, and that kind
    of knowledge is wisdom and nothing else. Which is why I knew
    few brave men. Either they are stupid and do not know what is
    right. Or they know what is right and cannot bring themselves to
    do it. Or they know what is right and do it, but do not feel and
    understand the fear that must be overcome. It takes a special
    man. Courage is more than the charge. More than dying or suf-
    fering the loss of a love in silence or being gallant. It is tempera-
    ment and, more, wisdom . . . ." How does O'Brien define courage
    in the form of the actions of his fellow soldiers and himself?

9. O'Brien writes: "In return for all your terror, the prairies stretch
    out, arrogantly unchanged." How does O'Brien describe the
    homecoming of the Vietnam veteran?

10. How is O'Brien different when he returns home than he was
    before he went to Vietnam? What experiences were most impor-
    tant in changing him?

Illumination Rounds by Larry R. Johannessen © 1992 NCTE.

17 Writing Based on an Interview

Select one of the writing options below. Then write a composition using the information gathered from the interview. Your finished composition should include references to ideas, views, or facts expressed by the interviewee.

1. Write a first-person, oral history account like the ones read and discussed in class. Make sure that it is written from the point of view of the person interviewed by the class. You should include an introduction to the account which establishes the context of the account and gives pertinent information about the interviewee. Make sure that in the final version, related ideas are grouped together, your questions have been edited out, and extraneous material is excluded.

2. Write a letter to a person of your choosing that is based on the interview. Include information about what was discussed, the circumstances of the interview, and your personal reactions. You might want to focus on what you learned about the Vietnam War, particularly in human terms.

3. Write a news or news-feature story based on the in-class interview. Try to capture the reader's attention in the opening sentence and immediately set the direction and tone of the story. Use the basic reporters' questions (who, what, when, where, why, and how) in organizing and writing your story.

Illumination Rounds by Larry R. Johannessen © 1992 NCTE.

18 Oral History Reading Guide: From *Everything We Had* by Al Santoli

Al Santoli's *Everything We Had* is a collection of oral histories gathered from veterans of the Vietnam War. An oral history is an edited transcription of a person's speech. To do an oral history, the interviewer must ask the interviewee questions, tape-record the answers, and then transcribe and edit the speech onto paper. As you read the selections handed out, think about the questions below. When you have finished reading the selections, answer the questions below. Be prepared to explain your answers in a class discussion.

1. What conclusions can you draw about the Vietnam War from the perspective of the soldiers and nurse from these oral histories?

2. How are these selections similar to short stories? How are they different?

3. How would you describe the tone of these selections?

4. How would you describe the language of the speakers of these selections?

5. What types of questions would the interviewer have had to ask in order to get these stories?

Illumination Rounds by Larry R. Johannessen © 1992 NCTE.

19 *In Country* by Bobbie Ann Mason: Study Guide Questions

1. Why does Sam live with her maternal uncle rather than with her mother? What are the causes of the problems between Sam and her mother?

2. What is the nature of the relationship between Sam and Emmett? How do they relate to each other? How does Sam treat Emmett, and vice versa? In what ways is their relationship different or unique for a teenager and an adult?

3. Why is Emmett unsuccessful in getting a job? Why is he unsuccessful in having a relationship with Anita? Why does he seem to have difficulty entering adult life?

4. What are the problems of Vietnam veterans as shown in this novel? In answering, consider these characters: Pete, Tom, Emmett, Buddy Mangrum, Jim, and Earl.

5. Why has the author included current problems of Sam's peers—Dawn and Lonnie—in this novel? What do they show about how the world has and has not changed since the days of Sam's father's youth?

6. Why is Sam infatuated with and drawn to Tom, although he is much older than she?

7. What is Sam's reaction to reading her father's journal? Is her reaction reasonable? Why or why not?

8. Why does she go to the woods/Cawood's pond? What experiences does she have there? What emotional reactions does she have? How does Emmett react to her having gone there?

9. What is the signficance of Sam's finding her own name on the wall (Vietnam Veterans Memorial)?

10. What is Emmett's reaction to the family visit to the Vietnam Veterans Memorial? What does this reaction suggest about his future?

Illumination Rounds by Larry R. Johannessen © 1992 NCTE.

20 *In Country* by Bobbie Ann Mason: Overall Questions

1. Part of the hero's quest is finding his or her own identity. As Sam studies her father's face in the photograph, she thinks, "The dead took their secrets with them. She wondered how far to go in honoring the dead if the dead offer you nothing except a little mindless protection by keeping their secrets from you. . . . [I]t almost seemed that he was playing a joke on her, a guessing game, as if he were saying, 'Know me if you can'" (182–83). To what extent is Sam's obsession with the Vietnam War in general and her father in particular a "hero's quest"?

2. At one point Sam thinks, "If it were up to women, there wouldn't be any war. No. That was a naive thought. When women got power, they were just like men. . . . What would make people want to kill? How did the Army get boys to do that? Why was there war" (208–09)? What does Mason suggest as the reason for war? (Consider the idea of power, the romance of battle, the concept of protecting home and family.)

3. Much of this novel has to do with the difference between fantasy and reality. For example, Sam idealizes her parents' brief marriage. Emmett and his veteran friends went off to war with glamorous ideas of war. Sam dreams of leaving her small town and working in Disneyworld or dancing with Bruce Springsteen. How does the author portray the "real world" as opposed to the world as the characters in the novel would like it to be?

4. The novel deals with important issues relating to the aftermath of the Vietnam War. According to the author, what are the effects on veterans, on their families, and, in particular, on the children of those who fought in the war?

5. Emmett says, "You can't do what we did and then be happy about it. And nobody lets you forget it" (222)! Yet at the end of the novel, we seem to have hope. In what ways is this a novel of reconciliation, both for Emmett and for the nation as a whole?

21 Vietnam War Novel: Images of War

Directions: Choose one of the following graphic assignments. In creating your graphic representation, strive for clarity, use of color, and creative imagery.

Theme: Pick one of the major themes in the novel and create a symbolic representation for that theme (such as the theme in Winston Groom's *Better Times Than These* that Americans are destroying themselves more than they are the enemy). Find quotations that support or demonstrate the theme. These quotations should appear in your graphic. Use color effectively in your graphic—color should have meaning and should show organization of ideas. Make sure that your graphic clearly shows what you think the author is saying about this theme.

Characterization: Create a graphic which plots the change in a character (such as Sam in Bobbie Ann Mason's *In Country*). Through your graphic, explore both the progress of and reasons for the change. Be certain that you visualize the "before," "during," and "after." Incorporate symbols, colors, direct quotes, and commentary to make your statement about how the character changes.

Character relationships: Create a graphic which plots the change in the relationship between two characters (such as the relationship between Cannonball and Bagger or Snake and Hodges in James Webb's *Fields of Fire*). Through your graphic, explore both the progress of and reasons for this change. Make certain that you visualize the stages in the relationship. Incorporate symbols, colors, direct quotes, and commentary to make your statement about the relationship.

Structure: Create a graphic which conveys your understanding of the structure of the novel (such as Stephen Wright's use of multiple points of view or cinematic cuts in *Meditations in Green*). Your graphic must contain visual representations of key scenes, episodes, or other important structural elements. Include significant quotations and commentary to make your statement about important structural elements.

Language: Create a graphic which conveys your interpretation of how the author uses language to convey meaning (such as Larry Heinemann's use of the Vietnam lexicon to convey meaning in *Close Quarters*). Your graphic should include visual symbols, color, and significant quotations to illustrate how the author uses language to convey meaning.

Illumination Rounds by Larry R. Johannessen © 1992 NCTE.

22 Character Analysis

Values:

1. Acceptance (Approval from others)
2. Achievement
3. Beauty
4. Companionship (Friendship)
5. Creativity
6. Health
7. Honesty
8. Independence
9. Justice
10. Knowledge
11. Love
12. Loyalty
13. Morality
14. Physical Appearance
15. Pleasure
16. Power
17. Recognition
18. Religious Faith
19. Self-respect
20. Skill
21. Tradition
22. Wealth

Character Analyzed _____

	Character's Values Early in the Work	If the Character Changes, Values Near the End
What does the character value *most*? List his or her top three values *in order*.	1. _____ 2. _____ 3. _____	1. _____ 2. _____ 3. _____
What does the character value *least*? List his or her bottom three values *in order*.	20. _____ 21. _____ 22. _____	20. _____ 21. _____ 22. _____

Be prepared to present *reasons* and *evidence* for your choices.

Illumination Rounds by Larry R. Johannessen © 1992 NCTE

23 Supporting Interpretations

Part A: The following is a list of possible evidence that a student has generated to support an interpretation of the character of Senator. The student who wrote this interpretation ranked health as Senator's No. 1 value. Circle the number of statements that would provide *specific* and *persuasive* evidence for this interpretation. Which of these are not specific and/or persuasive? Explain your responses.

Interpretation: During his first few months in Vietnam, Senator (Goodrich) values his health above all else.

1. "He's scared to death of walking point. He's scared to death of everything. He let Burgie die," Snake tells Baby Cakes (p. 239).

2. Senator says that it is stupid to do something for somebody else because all that it means is that you end up dying for another fool who is dying for you (p. 201).

3. Senator tells the mamasan that he accidentally shot, ". . . I'm really sorry. Really. . . . I should have looked more closely. I was scared. It was crazy to shoot like that" (p. 99).

4. Senator does not help other Marines who need help (p. 142).

5. When the enemy opens fire, Senator hugs the ground against the dike. Snake is caught in the open, writhing on the ground. "Die for Snake because Snake is out there dying for me? Makes no sense," Senator thinks (p. 202).

6. Snake tells Hodges, "Senator's pissed off again. Kersey came down and told me to put a team in the treeline. The one on the other side. I sent Senator. You shoulda heard him bitch and moan" (p. 2).

Part B: Each of the following quotations or examples could be used to support the interpretation below. After each, in a sentence or two, explain how it supports this interpretation. Your sentences should be written so that they could be included in a paragraph of evidence supporting the writer's understanding of the character of Senator.

Interpretation: During his first few months in Vietnam, Senator (Goodrich) values morality above all else.

1. After Senator shoots the mamasan, he is wary about shooting. On a patrol near an isolated village, he will not shoot at the fleeing enemy. Hodges tells him to "put out rounds." Goodrich replies, "Those are kids lieutenant. Kids and mamasans." Hodges again orders him to fire. So he thinks to himself, "He can court-martial me for not shooting, but he can't court-martial me for being a lousy shot" (p. 157).

2. When the team decides to kill the man and woman who may be responsible for killing two of their friends on Go Noi Island, Goodrich refuses to go along with it. Snake says, "Well, Senator. We're gonna do what we think we have to. You do what you think you have to." The narrator writes that "Goodrich walked quickly away. He heard Snake count behind him. . . . Shots cut through the heavy air. A lot of shots. Goodrich held his head. He felt wronged, humiliated. He had told them not to and they had not listened" (p. 294).

3. Senator says of the children he sees at the Village of Phu Phong (4), "I just can't help feeling sorry for them. . . . I still can't help it. . . . None of this is *their* fault" (pp. 90–91).

4. While on patrol in Nam An (2), Senator fires upon "a pajama-clad figure" he sees rustling about "on the porch of a burnt-out hootch" and wounds a village woman. Even though Snake tells him that "it's her own fault," Senator insists that he "should have looked more closely. . . . It was crazy to shoot like that" (pp. 98–99).

24 Composition Planning Sheet

Assignment: Select either the character of Hodges, Snake, or Senator (Goodrich) and write a composition in which you explain how the character's values change and why. Before attempting to formulate a thesis statement or write your composition, fill out the "Character Analysis" sheet as a guide and complete this planning sheet. In formulating your thesis statement, you might explain what the character values most in the beginning of the novel, what the character values most at or near the end, and the reason(s) for the change in values.

Sample Thesis:

At the beginning of James Webb's *Fields of Fire*, Lieutenant Robert E. Lee Hodges values honor, but after months in the bush leading his platoon, he is more concerned with loyalty to his men.

YOUR THESIS:

_____

_____

_____

List *specific* evidence for the character's top value at the beginning.

EVIDENCE	EXPLANATION of how the evidence supports the thesis

List *specific* evidence for the character's top value at or near the end.

EVIDENCE	EXPLANATION of how the evidence supports the thesis

Explain what *causes* this change in values and list supporting *evidence*.

Illumination Rounds by Larry R. Johannessen © 1992 NCTE.

25 Check Sheet

Name of writer _____

Name of evaluator(s) _____

_____

_____

1. Does the writer have a clearly stated thesis that follows the directions of the assignment?   Yes   No

2. Does the writer provide at least 3 pieces of specific, convincing evidence for the character's top value at the beginning?   Yes   No

3. Does the writer clearly explain how each piece of evidence supports his or her thesis?   Yes   No

4. Does the writer provide at least 3 pieces of specific, convincing evidence for the character's top value at the end?   Yes   No

5. Does the writer clearly explain how each piece of evidence supports his or her thesis?   Yes   No

6. Does the writer explain the reason(s) for the character's change in values?   Yes   No

7. Does the writer provide specific evidence to support what he or she gives as reasons for the change?   Yes   No

8. Reread the paper and mark any places where you think the writer needs to correct spelling, punctuation, capitalization, usage, etc.

9. What arguments can you think of that might be used against this writer's thesis?

Illumination Rounds by Larry R. Johannessen © 1992 NCTE.

Author

Larry R. Johannessen is assistant professor of English and director of English education at Saint Xavier University in Chicago, Illinois. During the Vietnam War, he served four years in the Marines, including over twenty months in Vietnam with 1st Reconnaissance Battalion, 1st Marine Division. He taught high school English and history for twelve years and has directed workshops and inservice programs for teachers in writing, thinking, and literature instruction. He was a participant, representing secondary teachers, in the English Coalition Conference in 1987. He is coauthor of two popular NCTE publications: *Writing about Literature* (1984) and *Designing and Sequencing Prewriting Activities* (1982). In addition to writing several articles and chapters in books, he has contributed articles to journals of NCTE and its affiliates.